ORGANIZATIONAL ENTRY
Recruitment, Selection, and Socialization of Newcomers

JOHN P. WANOUS
Michigan State University

ORGANIZATIONAL ENTRY

Recruitment, Selection, and Socialization of Newcomers

ADDISON-WESLEY PUBLISHING COMPANY

Reading, Massachusetts • Menlo Park, California
London • Amsterdam • Don Mills, Ontario • Sydney

THE ADDISON–WESLEY SERIES ON MANAGING HUMAN RESOURCES

Series Editor: John P. Wanous, Michigan State University

Fairness in Selecting Employees
Richard D. Arvey, University of Houston

Organizational Entry: Recruitment, Selection, and Socialization of Newcomers
John P. Wanous, Michigan State University

Increasing Productivity through Performance Appraisal
Gary P. Latham, University of Washington, and Kenneth N. Wexley, University of Akron

Managing Conflict at Organizational Interfaces
David Brown, Case-Western Reserve University

Library of Congress Cataloging In Publication Data

Wanous, John P
   Organizational entry.

   (Addison-Wesley series on managing human resources)
   Bibliography: p.
   Includes indexes.
   1.   Recruiting of employees.   2.   Employee selection.
3.   Discrimination in employment.   I.   Title.   II.   Series.
HF5549.5.R44W36   658.31'1   79-6274
ISBN 0-201-08456-2

ISBN-0-201-08456-2
ABCDEFGHIJ-AL-89876543210

Foreword

Widespread attention given to the effective management of human resources came of age in the 1970s. As we enter the 1980s, the importance placed on it continues to grow. Personnel departments, which used to be little more than the keepers of employee files, are now moving to the forefront in corporate visibility.

The difficulties encountered in effective human resource management are without parallel. Surveys of managers and top level executives consistently show "human problems" at the top of most lists. The influx of the behavioral sciences into business school programs is further testimony to the active concern now placed on human resources as a critical element in organizational effectiveness.

The primary objective of this Addison-Wesley series is to articulate new solutions to chronic human resource problems; for example, the selection and entry of newcomers, performance appraisal, and conflict management. The aim is to communicate with a variety of audiences, including present managers, students as future managers, and fellow professionals in business, government, and academia.

John P. Wanous
Series Editor

Preface

This book is the culmination of my interest, which began about 1970, in newcomers to organizations. At that time my interest in, and knowledge of, the study of newcomers was limited primarily to the main thrust of my doctoral dissertation—an experimental comparison between a realistic job preview and traditional company recruiting methods to hire telephone operators. Following this I completed a two-year project on the entry of new students into MBA programs in several different graduate schools of business administration. It was about then that the term "organizational entry" seemed to best describe my research interests.

In the middle 1970s I became convinced that there were several consistent experiences that are common for almost all newcomers to organizations. This increased my own motivation to define organizational entry as a worthwhile topic for researchers to investigate and for organizations to recognize. It seemed appropriate to share this conviction with both academic and business audiences. In 1975 I published two articles in periodicals read by those in business. The message was to seriously consider changing to realistic job previews as a way to recruit newcomers. This message is repeated in Chapters 2 and 3. On the academic side, the most immediate predecessor to this book is a literature review article published in 1977.

It should now be clear that my intention in this book is to address several audiences. Thus the focus of the book changes from chapter to chapter, and sometimes within a chapter itself. The book is aimed at three audiences: students, academics, and personnel managers. For the students I try to describe what it's like to go through the recruitment selection, organizational choice, and socialization stages of entry into a new organization. Students are likely to find some useful information in each of the chapters to help prepare them for future organizational entry.

Trying to satisfy both students and academics is difficult because students may find too many technical terms in some parts of the book, whereas academics may find too few. I have tried to write at a level understandable and interesting to a general audience. To satisfy the academic audience, I have added references throughout the text. Those who want to pursue certain topics in greater detail should have sufficient leads to begin a literature search.

Finally, this book is addressed to personnel managers in various types of organizations. I have not limited the discussion to business because the research shows common experiences for newcomers across different types of organizations. The primary message to this group is to consider changing to realistic recruitment. I have tried to explain the logic of traditional versus realistic recruitment, the expected results from each, and the conditions conducive to each. Chapters 2 and 3 will probably be most useful for this audience.

Besides the intellectual attraction of studying organizational entry, my interest in the topic goes to a deeper, more personal level. Changing organizations has had a significant impact both on my professional and personal life: leaving one graduate school to complete the Ph.D. at another, choosing one university over another for a first academic job, and leaving the first job for a second university. In each of these changes I became acquainted with practically all of the topics covered in this book on a firsthand basis. This book is, thus, also an attempt to make sense out of these transitions for myself by writing about them.

I began to write this book about two years ago. While I was writing it, several people have helped in various ways. Ed Lawler, Tim Hall, and Ben Schneider each encouraged me to undertake the book project. The Graduate School of Business at Michigan State University helped enormously by providing me with released time from teaching duties. Janina Latack and Neal Schmitt at Michigan State provided very helpful comments on early drafts. The Management Department's secretaries were somehow able to read my handwriting and produce a clearly typed manuscript, literally overnight. Linda Penrose, Kathy Jegla, Claire Rammel, and Maryalice Frantz have my gratitude for doing such a marvelous job, and remaining extremely good-natured throughout.

At the later stages of this project, Ben Schneider, Jim Walker, and Edgar Schein reviewed the entire manuscript. Their comments were extremely useful in guiding the final revisions.

East Lansing, Michigan   J. P. W.
November 1979

Contents

What Is Organizational Entry?

1

Organizational entry includes the wide variety of events occurring when new members join organizations. By its very nature the entry process must be considered from the perspective of both the individual and the organization. Individuals choose organizations, and organizations select newcomers from among applicants.

Organizational entry concerns movement into and out of businesses, schools, the armed forces, etc. Because of the focus on crossing the boundary, the immediate concern of organizational entry is to identify those factors affecting these moves. To put this another way, March and Simon (1958) distinguished between the decision to *participate* in an organization and the decision to *perform* well in that organization. This is a book about participation, not performance. *Both* the individual and organizational viewpoints are considered; March and Simon focused mostly on the individual's choice to stay or leave.

The purpose of Chapter 1 is to introduce readers to various issues in organizational entry and to argue for the importance of studying this particular "slice" of their working careers. A hypothetical "case study" based on a composite of typical entry experiences is presented next. It is used to illustrate key issues that are themselves the subjects for more intensive treatment in later chapters. After this is done, examples are given to show how expensive and inefficient the entry process can be to an organization.

The final objective of this chapter is to present a schematic model of organizational entry that shows the major factors and how they relate to each other. This model serves as a common reference point throughout the book. Since it will be referred to in each chapter, the reader is advised to study it well.

A CASE STUDY OF ENTRY

Ed enjoyed "working with people." His choice of psychology as a major seemed consistent to him as a way of furthering his understanding of other people. Even though psychology was a popular college major in the 1970s, Ed soon learned that most companies were interested in those who had majored in business administration. So, Ed went east to get an MBA, after first graduating from a state university in the midwest. In graduate business school he chose management and marketing as areas for concentrated study. He had always felt more comfortable with "qualitative" subjects than he did with "quantitative" ones such as math, accounting, finance, or economics.

During his second year of the MBA program, Ed interviewed six different companies on campus, and was invited back to three of them for further assessment. Prior to the campus interviews he had gone to a couple of "crash courses" that the school offered on how to prepare for job interviews. He was given pointers on what to wear, what questions to expect, what questions to ask, and what information about the company he should obtain. At the end of the courses, he participated in a "mock interview" before a videotape machine. He saw himself on TV (for the first time) and carefully listened to the "pointers" given him by the instructor. By the time Ed went to his first interview, he felt prepared. He had talked with other students about their experiences, read the three most recent annual reports for each company, and rehearsed answers to the "open-ended" questions he anticipated.

Fortunately for Ed, two companies offered him a job as a "management trainee." There were differences between the two positions in terms of geographical location, starting salary, general reputation as a desirable place for the new college graduates, and initial job assignment. After weighing all these factors, Ed accepted the position with a very large, multinational corporation that sold business machines as its main product. He would begin with them in their sales training program in June, about two weeks after graduation.

Ed's long-term goal was to enter general management rather than to spend his whole career in sales. However, in this particular company, going into sales was regarded by most as the fastest route to district level management. (To go higher than that would require a strong background on the financial side of the corporation, but Ed was unaware of this at the point of his entry into the new job.)

By the time Ed began his first day at work, the company had spent $1,575 in direct and indirect costs. The rough breakdown is shown in Table 1.1.

TABLE 1.1

Printed material, posters, ads	$ 25
Campus recruitment interview	50
First trip to company (travel, food)	400
Assessment center* costs for first trip	600
Second trip to company (travel, food)	400
Miscellaneous indirect costs (letters, phone calls, processing of forms)	100
Total	$1,575

*The assessment center was an intensive three-day session in which Ed and other new recruits participated in simulated management experiences, e.g., organizing a day's work, writing letters and memos, making phone calls, working in a group to make a decision. The assessment center as a selection technique is described in greater detail in Chapter 5.

The initial training period lasted about three months and was held away from corporate headquarters (and the field offices, too) in a special campus-like location devoted to "corporate training and management development." Most of those Ed met either were other newcomers or were from the Human Resources staff assigned to this location. Although the program was well conceived, organized, and interesting, Ed felt that he still hadn't learned "how things really work" in the company. The next six months of initial field sales experience helped to correct this deficiency. During this period Ed was placed under the mentorship of an experienced sales representative.

After the nine-month mark Ed was on his own in the field. Up to this point he had received some feedback about his performance during the training sessions, and his field mentor made a formal appraisal prior to Ed's solo run. Now, however, things were quite different. For the first nine months, Ed had been on a straight salary. Now, he was on a small base salary plus sales commission. The formula for computing it was fairly complicated, and had one striking feature. If a company decided not to renew a machine rental contract, a portion of the lost revenue was "charged back" to the sales division and subtracted from Ed's commission. This was designed to force sales personnel to give good, attentive service to their customers. In practice, however, some decisions to terminate rentals were completely out of the control of the sales person. This meant that Ed's income was not as predictable as it had been. Further, Ed soon learned that the charge-back system was considered a threat by many new sales representatives and was resented by others. The full impact of this compensation system was completely unanticipated by Ed. The previous explanation given to him had seemed abstract at the time—living with this system was another matter altogether.

Up to the nine-month mark, Ed had cost the company $2,000 a month in salary, plus another $700 monthly in fringe benefits, for a total of $24,300. The recruitment cost added $1,575 to this. The training costs, which included the costs of maintaining the training facility, the fees of outside consultants used, and the salaries of all those employed by the company at the training and development center, were about $5,000 more. Thus the company had spent over $30,000 on Ed in only nine months in exchange for no tangible return.

After about six months in the field, Ed left for another company. During the six months before leaving he had made a few small deals, but did not generate more than $3,000 a month—barely enough to "cover" what he had been paid up to that point. In the six months since training Ed just barely paid his own way so that when he quit, the company was clearly out the $30,000 development cost spent in the first nine months. His leaving also meant that another $30,000 would have to be spent on his replacement—with no guarantee to the company that there would be a solid return on the next "human capital" investment.

ISSUES RAISED BY THE CASE STUDY

This short case of Ed's entry into his first job is a composite of many stories. By reviewing several elements of this case, a number of issues concerning *organizational entry* will be raised. This is a book about the entry of new people into organizations of all kinds—business, schools, armed forces. Although there are differences among these various types of organizations (and these differences will be pointed out), there are many more commonalities among them. Thus the entry process of new members into organizations is one that can be thought of as a *general* process in which the issues and events are remarkably similar among different organizations.

Issue 1: What Effect Did Vocational Choice Have on Ed's Decision to Leave the Company?

In the case study, Ed liked to "work with people." This could be an indication of a strong *affiliative* need (McClelland, Atkinson, Lowell, and Clark 1953). However, the job Ed took was in sales. The sales job is commonly regarded as an excellent vocational choice for one highly motivated by *achievement*, rather than by affiliation. This is because the sales job provides opportunities in three key psychological areas crucial to those who have strong needs for achievement. These people are (1) able to take personal responsibility for what is done, (2) able to set goals of moderate difficulty (neither too hard nor too easy), and (3) able to get concrete feedback on their own actions.

It is easy to say that Ed was not matched well to the sales job in this basic, vocational sense. Tracking down the reasons for this mismatch is, however, a much harder task. Ed could have been given poor advice by vocational counselors at school or he may have been given good advice that he chose to ignore. The company may have been partly responsible either for not recognizing Ed's vocational needs or for misdiagnosing them. Ed himself may have viewed the sales job as a convenient route to the top. He may have believed that he could gain his ultimate goal of general administration through a temporary stint in sales, without fully appreciating the costs of doing so. Vocational choice is discussed in Chapter 4.

Issue 2: How Did the Recruitment Process Affect Ed's Decision to Leave?

A number of recruitment issues are raised by this case. First, how much did Ed *really* know about the company prior to his acceptance of its job offer? His reaction to the sales commission method of compensation indicates that Ed was not fully informed in this key area. Issues surrounding what the typical outsider knows about the inner workings of an organization, and where the information comes from, will be raised in Chapters 2 and 3.

A second recruitment issue concerns the company itself. Why should it divulge negative information about itself to an outsider, even if the information is correct? Wouldn't this be suicide in a competitive labor market? How would competent newcomers ever be attracted to the company? And finally, isn't there plenty of time *after* newcomers are hired to let them in on how things really work on the inside? The issue of how much to tell job candidates during the recruitment process will be given extensive treatment in Chapters 2 and 3.

Issue 3: How Did Ed's Own Organizational Choice Affect His Decision to Leave?

Any entry into a new organization involves *two* choices. The organization must choose the candidate (called *selection* here) and the individual must accept it or reject it, (called *organizational choice* here). Several issues about Ed's organizational choice will be raised in this book. Did Ed make the "right" choice? What does the right choice mean? How did Ed actually make the choice; i.e., what was the decision process that resulted in his picking the company he did? Organizational choice is discussed in Chapter 4.

Issue 4: How Did the Company's Selection Process Affect Ed's Decision to Leave?

Before Ed was actually confronted with which job to take, he had to first be considered acceptable by the firm. What steps do organizations go through in (1) deciding what people they need for which jobs, (2) obtaining information about job candidates, and (3) actually making the selection decision? These three issues will be considered in Chapter 5 on selection.

An overriding issue for this company's selection process is what basic criteria were used in making the selection decision. If Ed's potential job *performance* only was considered, the lack of attention to Ed's *human needs* being congruent with the job climate could account for his dissatisfaction and early withdrawal from the company. The basic issue raised here is to what extent a job candidate's *needs* are matched to the organizational *climate* in the same way that the candidate's *abilities* are matched to the demands or *requirements of the job*. (See Fig. 1.1 on page 11.)

Issue 5: What Effect Did the Socialization Process Have on Ed's Decision to Leave?

Newcomers to this organization entered as a group and were kept together for the first three months apart from the rest of the organization. Those in the sales area were then assigned a mentor for six more months before being left to fend for themselves. Although organizations are remarkably similar in their recruitment practices and strategy, there is rather wide diversity in how they attempt to integrate newcomers after they enter. In Chapter 6 on organizational socialization, a category system is developed to organize all the various methods used. A "stage model" of typical newcomer experiences is constructed. Finally, several different socialization strategies are discussed, and four detailed case studies are presented to illustrate the diversity of socialization experiences. The reader will see, secondhand, what it's like to be a new police officer, an army recruit, a first-year student in graduate business school, and a management trainee.

WHY THE STUDY OF ORGANIZATIONAL ENTRY IS IMPORTANT

The story of Ed's experience illustrates one important reason why considerable attention is and should be placed on the entry of new organization members—the cost of "premature" turnover is quite high. It takes a while for almost all organizations to get newcomers to "pay their own way." The costs vary widely from job to job and organization to organization, but there are *always* costs—even for the lowest level, lowest paid jobs. For example, in an insurance company the replacement cost has been estimated to be $6,000 for a claims investigator, $24,000 for a field examiner, $31,600 for a sales person (with *below* average performance!) and $185,100 for a sales manager (Flamholtz 1972).[1] These replacement-cost figures include such items as acquiring a new person, training, and moving the present holder to another organization or to another position. The United States Navy estimates that it costs $30,000 to obtain a naval officer through the ROTC, $86,000 for one via the Naval Academy, and $1,500,000 for a competent fighter pilot.[2] If a top-quality Ph.D. research scientist leaves an organization such as Bell Labs or DuPont Labs, it can cost that organization $100,000 to $200,000 if the person was a newcomer and didn't remain more than two years. A telephone company estimated the replacement cost for a newly hired operator who left within the first six months to be about $3,500. At one time this company was hiring about 100 operators per month merely to compensate for the loss of operators who left the organization.

The fact that turnover is expensive is certainly a good reason to look more carefully at entry from the individual's viewpoint. This conclusion is further reinforced by also recognizing that the *highest turnover rates are found among the newly hired employees.* Most companies calculate turnover rates as a percentage. For example, if a small manufacturing company had a steady average work force of 500 employees throughout a full year, but hired 75 people during that period, the annual turnover rate for the whole company would be 15 percent. Such rates can also be calculated for departments or smaller units within the organization, and they can be calculated for particular groups of employees based on sex, age, race, or how new they are to the organization. For example, some companies calculate the turnover rates for new MBAs hired. When calculated on a basis other than the total organization, rates can be quite high—often over 100 percent per year within particular types of jobs, or other subgroup.

The experience of one telephone company with its operators serves as a good example. During the late 1960s and early 1970s, a period of strong economic activity nationwide, there was a companywide turnover rate for operators of about 30 to 35 percent. However, when the company looked only at the newcomers who had been employed for less than six

---

[1] Recent increases in the cost of living must also be taken into account, since these costs were calculated in 1972.

[2] As of 1977 according to Dr. Robert Morrison in personal communication.

TABLE 1.2

Turnover rates for newcomers to organizations

TIME PERIOD	PERCENT WHO LEFT DURING PERIOD	CUMULATIVE PERCENT
Weeks 1–4	33.5	33.5
5–8	9.7	43.2
9–12	6.9	50.1
13–16	1.7	51.8
17–20	2.3	54.1
21–24	1.0	55.1
25–28*	2.3	57.4[†]

* A total of 1,736 persons was tracked for 29 weeks. Of this group, 1,239 left and only 497 remained at work longer than 28 weeks.

[†] Since over 57 percent left in only six months, the *annual* turnover rate for this group of newcomers is about 115 percent.

Source: J. P. Wanous, S. A. Stumpf, and H. Bedrosian, 1978. *Turnover of New Employees*. Paper presented at the annual meeting of the Academy of Management, San Francisco.

months, the annual rate was 150 percent! A recent study of new job placements through the New York State Employment Service (Wanous, Stumpf, and Bedrosian 1978) clearly shows that the highest turnover rates are for newcomers. Table 1.2 shows the percentage of new hires who dropped out during each of seven time periods of four weeks each. Although these data come from only one study, the persons included were placed in a wide variety of jobs and organizations throughout the entire state.

Historically, the field of industrial psychology has viewed entry from an *organizational* perspective that concerns the questions surrounding the matching of a job candidate's abilities to organizational job requirements. Even a recent 1,740-page "handbook" on the state of the art did not systematically examine entry from the *individual's* viewpoint (Dunnette 1976). The topics covered in that handbook relevant for entry were (1) the meaning and measurement of aptitudes, skills, and abilities; (2) personality and personality assessment; (3) job and task analysis; (4) recruitment, selection, and job placement; (5) training; and (6) vocational preferences. With the exception of the last area, the first five all concern the entry of newcomers from the perspective of the hiring organization. What is missing is a *balanced* view of entry; one that discusses the issues from both viewpoints and treats the material side by side. This book is the first such systematic coverage of *organizational entry.*[3] The uniqueness of this approach is in *adding* the individual's viewpoint to our existing store of knowledge on entry from the organizational vantage point.

A MODEL OF MATCHING INDIVIDUALS AND ORGANIZATIONS

A major theme in the examination of the entry process is the "matching" of individual and organization. A model of this process is shown here and will be referred to repeatedly throughout the entire book.

Figure 1.1 is based on the Minnesota studies of *vocational* adjustment (Lofquist and Dawis 1969) that has been changed to an *organizational* focus rather than an occupational theme. It shows two ways in which individuals and organizations get matched to each other. The top half of the diagram shows that the abilities of an individual are matched to the organization's job requirements. This matching process is the traditional view of organizational selection. The major consequence of a *mis*match is also shown in terms of job performance at work. Over the years the concern of matching people and organizations has been most often expressed as the top half of this figure. Clearly, this represents the viewpoint of the organization rather than that of the individual.

In contrast, the lower part of the figure shows a second type of matching process, that between the *needs* of human beings and the capacity of the organization to *reinforce* those needs. The impact of a mismatch is on job *satisfaction* and *commitment* to the organization, rather than on the level of job *performance*. This view, therefore, is that of the individual, since the focus is on personal needs satisfaction rather than on job performance.

Having shown this general model, several questions still remain. First, what is meant by needs as compared to abilities? Second, what is the factual basis for the probable impact of each type of mismatch? Third, can a

---

[3] Others have examined occupational or career entry issues in a balanced way (Hall 1976; Schein 1978; Van Maanen 1977). This book is a parallel attempt at a closely related, but distinct, topic.

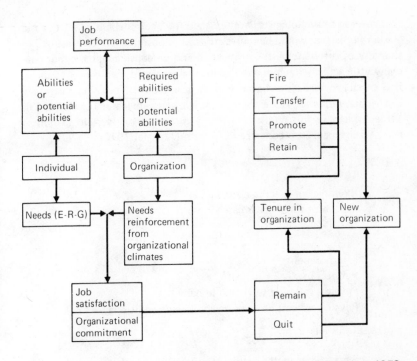

Fig. 1.1 *Matching individual and organization. (From J. P. Wanous, 1978, Realistic job previews: Can a procedure to reduce turnover also influence the relationship between abilities and performance?* Personnel Psychology *31: 250. Reprinted by permission.)*

mismatch at the "top" of Fig. 1.1 also affect job satisfaction and commitment. Can a mismatch at the "bottom" influence job performance?

Needs versus Abilities and Potential

Human needs represent the basic strivings or desires of people, whereas human abilities refer to what people are able to do *now* or are potentially able to do in the *future*. Given this distinction, it is easy to see that the primary concern of individuals is needs satisfaction, whereas organizations are typically more concerned with a person's abilities than with a person's satisfaction.

For years psychologists have searched for a comprehensive set of basic human needs that would be representative of most people. This resulted in a variety of different "lists" of what should be considered basic, but relatively little agreement among the various investigators who proposed them. It is crucial to realize, however, that the term "needs" refers to a *category* of specific *outcomes,* rather than to a single concrete factor (Lawler 1973). Table 1.3 shows this relationship for a three-category system of human needs: Existence, Relatedness, and Growth (Alderfer 1972).

TABLE 1.3

Examples of specific outcomes
in each of three needs categories

EXISTENCE NEEDS

Salary level
Fringe benefits
Fairness in pay
Physical safety at work and in daily life
Physical aspects of working and living conditions

RELATEDNESS NEEDS

Work or live with friendly people
Get respect from others (customers, friends, co-workers)
Get support from other people
Remain open in communications with others
Desire feeling of prestige from others

GROWTH NEEDS

Degree of challenge at work or at leisure
Desire for activities in which you are independent
Degree that your abilities are used to their fullest
Personal involvement at work
Feeling of self-esteem

The three-category system, E-R-G for short, is of relatively recent origin, and seems to be in accord with the data accumulated over the last decade (Alderfer 1972; Wahba and Bridwell 1976; Wanous and Zwany 1977). For the sake of comparison, Fig. 1.2 shows how E-R-G compares with the well-known, five-category system proposed by Maslow (1943).

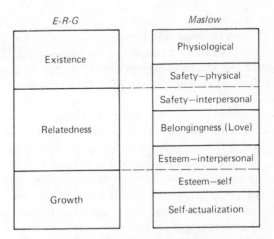

Fig. 1.2 *Comparison of Maslow and E-R-G needs categories.*

The advantage in using E-R-G is that each of the three categories refers to a different focus or orientation of the individual. For example, Existence needs refer to one's desire for material things—a very tangible type of need. Relatedness needs refer to one's posture with other people; the whole host of interpersonal relationships is included here. Finally, Growth needs refer to an inward orientation toward one's self.

Having defined needs, let us now contrast them with human abilities. Abilities refer to those mental, physical, or interpersonal activities that a person can do at the present time. They represent what the individual has already learned how to do. In contrast, potential abilities refer to what some call an *aptitude* (Anastasi 1968). A typing test would reveal how well I can actually type now, whereas a test of finger dexterity and hand–eye coordination would indicate my potential as a typist, should I try to improve my present ability.

What Is the Factual Basis for the Impact of Mismatches in the Model?

The lower portion of Fig. 1.1 indicates that job *satisfaction* and *commitment* to the organization are directly affected by a mismatch between the individual's needs and the organization's capacity to satisfy those needs. This is actually a statement about what causes satisfaction at work, i.e., a *comparison* between what is desired and what is supplied (Wanous and Lawler 1972). Thus the most direct consequence of a mismatch is low job satisfaction, typically followed by quitting the organization. (See Fig. 4.3 for more detail.) The accumulated research evidence for this is quite strong (Mobley, Griffeth, Hand, and Meglino 1979; Porter and Steers 1973), and is discussed in Chapter 4.

A second possible reaction to a mismatch between human needs and organizational climate is a decrease in the *commitment* of the person to the organization, or a decrease in the degree of *identification* with it. Both commitment and identification have proven difficult to define precisely; there is no general agreement on their exact meaning. [See Hall and Rabinowitz (1977) for a review.] Dissatisfaction with one's job often causes one to quit an organization. On the other hand, commitment refers to one's overall attachment to an organization. It is certainly possible that those with high job satisfaction may quit anyway, if other (i.e., nonjob) aspects of the organization do fulfill basic needs. In fact, one study was able to isolate changes in commitment that resulted in managerial turnover (Porter, Crampon, and Smith 1976). In a comparison of those who eventually quit with those who stayed, they found no difference in organizational commitment six months prior to the actual quitting. However, within the last two months prior to the quit there was a significant difference in commitment between the leavers and the stayers. The decrease in commitment led to quitting.

The Matching Model thus lists both job satisfaction and organizational commitment as outcomes of the needs–climates match. Since an organization has many climates, rather than a single overall climate, it makes sense to keep these distinct (Schneider 1975). Thus job satisfaction refers to the match between a person's needs and the reinforcement received from the work performed in that organization. On the other hand, organizational commitment refers to the match between human needs and the reinforcement received from the nonjob climates of the organization, e.g., financial compensation, career opportunities, company policies, co-workers, etc.

It is interesting to note that absenteeism (a milder form of withdrawal from an organization) is *not* as strongly related to job satisfaction as was once believed (Nicholson, Brown, and Chadwick-Jones 1976). Early reviews of the literature on absenteeism and turnover (Brayfield and Crockett 1955; Herzberg, Mausner, Peterson, and Capwell 1957; Vroom 1964) all indicated a negative relationship between job satisfaction on the one hand, and turnover and absenteeism on the other.

A review of over 60 studies (Porter and Steers 1973) found evidence for the former negative link, but much weaker evidence for the impact on absenteeism. Part of the explanation for this is that fewer studies have concerned absenteeism. Another part of the explanation is that absenteeism has been measured in two ways, the number of *days* absent over a specified time period and the number of *occasions* of absence. Four straight days of absence count as only one occasion, but four consecutive Fridays away from work count as four occasions. This confusion has made it hard to compare different studies. The final part of the explanation is that most organizations can control absenteeism by enforcing rules against it, but they cannot force people to remain unwillingly. Thus it's not hard to see why one telephone campany was plagued with turnover, but had no absenteeism problem. Too many unexcused absences resulted in the loss of one's job, so people quit if they could, but came to work if they were unable to quit.

The top half of Fig. 1.1 shows that a mismatch between one's abilities (or potential) and the job requirements results in poor performance at work. The evidence for this link comes from years of research on the validity of selection procedures for predicting the future performance of job candidates. Ghiselli (1966) summarized all the available studies from 1920–1966 and concluded that it was easier to predict success in training programs than in actual on-the-job performance (average correlations of .29 versus .19).[4] In an update (Ghiselli 1973), the averages increased to a correlation of .39 for the prediction of training success and .22 for the prediction of job performance. Although positive and supportive of the

---

[4] A correlation is an index number used to show how closely two things are related to each other. It can have values of -1.00 to $+1.00$. A correlation of zero indicates no relationship at all between two things. Increases away from zero (in either a positive or negative direction) mean that two things *are* related to each other.

Matching Model presented here, these are *not* high correlations and indicate that many factors influence job performance other than just how well abilities are matched to job requirements. Employee *motivation* must be considered as having a major impact on job performance as well (Lawler 1973) as shown in Fig. 1.3. A detailed model of motivation is developed in Chapter 4 in the context of Organizational Choice.

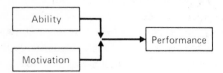

Fig. 1.3 *Determinants of employee job performance. If motivation is totally absent, performance is zero even if abilities are high. If abilities are zero (i.e., totally inappropriate to the task), performance is zero even if motivation is high.*

Research (Wanous, Stumpf, and Bedrosian 1978, 1979) was designed to test the connections shown in the Matching Model. To do so, it was first necessary to separate voluntary and involuntary turnover. Then measures of performance and satisfaction were obtained. According to the model, job satisfaction should be lower for those who quit voluntarily than it is for those who leave involuntarily, and this fact is what was found. Furthermore, job performance ratings by supervisors should be higher for those who stay in the organization or who leave voluntarily as compared with those who leave involuntarily. This was also found to be the case. Finally, there should be moderately strong relationships between job performance and involuntary turnover on the one hand, and job satisfaction and voluntary turnover on the other. This was also found to be true. While this is only one such study, it was based on a very large sample ($N = 1,736$) of workers throughout New York State.

Are There Other Consequences of Mismatches?

Can a mismatch between human needs and the organizational climate also have an impact on job performance? Can satisfaction be influenced by a mismatch between capabilities and job requirements? The answer in both cases is yes, in some instances. Since these examples are less frequent than those shown in Fig.1.1, these linkages are omitted from the model and discussed here instead.

Most studies of mismatches between needs and climates (i.e., low commitment and job dissatisfaction) focus on their probable influences on turnover and absenteeism. Many have also been concerned with job performance, however. In fact much of management theory has been preoccupied with the possible link between job satisfaction and performance, which has been unfortunate. [See Schwab and Cummings (1970) for a review of this history.]

Contrary to what many people believe to be true, there is *no consistently strong relationship,* either positive or negative, between job satisfaction and performance (Brayfield and Crockett 1955; Vroom 1964). Despite the fact that there is no trend one way or the other, satisfaction and performance may be linked in a particular organization (e.g., Wanous 1974) or in a specific situation (Cherrington, Reitz, and Scott 1971). Chris Argyris (1964) has done a good job of identifying instances in which low satisfaction resulted in the employee's poor performance as a way of retaliating against the organization that is the cause of the dissatisfaction. Sometimes this can go to extremes, e.g., sabotage.

When abilities and job requirements are mismatched, turnover can result. This is most likely to occur when the individual is *over*qualified for a job, rather than underqualified. In this case quitting is the most likely result depending on the number of available jobs elsewhere. As an example, a telephone company used to have the operator-hiring policy of wanting college graduates or those with at least some college experience. This policy was relaxed when it became clear that operators with too much education were difficult to retain. This example also serves to reinforce the usefulness of the Matching Model. Had this company taken the comprehensive view of entry illustrated in Fig. 1.1, it would not have required its operators to have so much education. The company's focus on job performance led it to the "more is better" policy regarding education, and prevented it from realizing the policy's potential impact on turnover. Had the company recognized that overqualified operators might be also mismatched in terms of needs and organizational climate, it might have avoided costly turnover problems. It took the company about two years to get that policy changed, and then turnover was lowered.

CONCLUSIONS

1. Organizational entry is a two-sided process in which individuals choose organizations and organizations select individuals. It is thus similar to the study of careers, or vocational entry, but refers to a much smaller part of one's total working life.

2. It is important to study the entry of newcomers to organizations because the exit of valued employees is very expensive. Not all turnover is costly, however, since it is clearly desirable to have poor performers leave. Thus it is important to distinguish between voluntary and involuntary turnover.

3. The entry process can be represented schematically as a *dual matching process*. One match is between the individual's needs and the capacity of the organizational climates to reinforce them. The direct consequence of this match is on job satisfaction, and, indirectly on voluntary turnover. The other match is between the individual's present and future abilities, and the requirements of a particular job. The direct consequence of this match is on job performance, and indirectly on involuntary turnover.

THE PLAN OF THIS BOOK

The chapters that follow can be divided into three broad "stages" of the entry process. The next two chapters focus on recruitment as part of the *preentry* stage. In Chapter 2, it will be seen that outsiders to organizations really know very little about them. Two philosophies of recruitment are contrasted, traditional and realistic, and a preference for the latter expressed. In Chapter 3, the second chapter on recruitment, how to do realistic recruitment is described in detail. Results from organizations using realism are summarized. In these two chapters on recruitment the perspectives of the individual and organization are both taken into account.

The second stage, *entry*, contains two more chapters. The first of these, Chapter 4, is written primarily from the perspective of the newcomer individual; it concerns how one makes the choice to join a new organization. Chapter 5, however, is written from an organizational viewpoint; it focuses on how newcomers are selected for job offers by organizations. Finally, Chapter 6 concerns organizational socialization of newcomers, a *postentry* topic.

Organizational Recruitment

2

Recruitment is examined from the dual perspective of the individual and the organization. This chapter is divided into five parts, each of which will (1) show the relationship of recruitment to the entry model already developed, (2) identify conflicts between individuals and organizations during recruitment, (3) describe what "outsider" individuals really know about organizations, (4) show the sources used by organizations to find newcomers, and (5) differentiate between two very different philosophies of recruitment. The following chapter, Realistic Recruitment, goes into greater depth and detail about how realistic recruitment has been done in several organizations.

RELATIONSHIP OF RECRUITMENT TO
THE MODEL OF ORGANIZATIONAL ENTRY

In Chapter 1, the Matching Model of individual and organization was presented (Fig. 1.1). Two different types of matchings were shown: (1) between abilities (and/or potential abilities) *and* organizational job requirements, and (2) between individual needs *and* organizational climates. Keeping these two matchings separate, it can be argued that *recruitment* has its greatest impact on the latter matching, while *selection* (Chapter 5) has its greatest effect on the former matching. By following the Matching Model, it can be further seen that the effectiveness of *recruitment* can be best assessed by examining employee job satisfaction, organizational commitment, and voluntary turnover. On the other hand, the effectiveness of *selection* methods is better judged by examining the job performance and involuntary turnover of new employees.

It is, however, overly simplistic to treat the twin matchings as existing separately from each other, because they are closely linked. The twin processes of matching individual and organization are interrelated due to a rather high degree of tension that constantly exists between them. The best way to describe the organizational entry process is to think of it as "individuals and organizations attracting and selecting each other" (Porter, Lawler, and Hackman 1975, p. 131).

CONFLICTS DURING ORGANIZATIONAL ENTRY

One of the clearest statements about the conflicts surrounding the dual nature of choice during organizational entry can be found in the work of Porter, Lawler, and Hackman (1975). Figure 2.1 summarizes the four types of conflict they have identified.

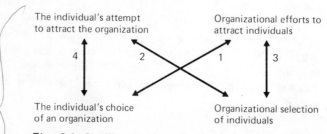

Fig. 2.1 *Conflicts during organizational entry. (From L. W. Porter, E. E. Lawler, III, and R. J. Hackman, 1975, Behavior in Organizations, p. 134. Reprinted by permission of the McGraw-Hill Book Company.)*

Two of the conflicts (numbers 1 and 2) occur between individuals and organizations. Type 1 occurs because individuals need to have complete information about an organization, and the information needs to be accurate. Without such information, the individual cannot make a very wise choice, i.e., one that matches needs with organizational climates. The conflict occurs because typical actions by organizations to attract, or recruit, newcomers do *not* (1) give *full* information (usually they give only information that is positive), and do *not* (2) give *accurate* information (sometimes the descriptions are biased by recruiters).[1]

The second conflict between individual and organization occurs for many of the same reasons as the first. Most individuals feel that it's important to generate as many job offers as possible, in an attempt to obtain one that will be highly desirable. Because of this desire, individuals are not prone to disclose their own shortcomings in terms of abilities, and quite often describe their desired job in terms of what they think the organization has to offer (rather than in terms of what they would really prefer).

The last two conflicts are internal to either the organization or the individual. The third conflict indicates that recruitment efforts may hinder effective selection of new personnel. The goals of any personnel input function are to *both select* competent people *and* to *retain* them. Thus typical recruitment practices that emphasize information limited only to the positive aspects of the organization may result in a mismatch between human needs and organizational climate, as shown in the Matching Model (Fig. 1.1). The fourth kind of conflict can be explained in somewhat the same fashion. When individuals misrepresent themselves to appear more attractive to an organization, they run the risk of being offered jobs ill suited to their own skills and needs. The individual's final choice of a job depends on those that are actually offered. Therefore, an individual's efforts to appear overly attractive do influence *which* jobs are offered. Consequently, the individual's own choice of organization is limited to those that offer admittance.

WHAT DO "OUTSIDER" INDIVIDUALS KNOW ABOUT ORGANIZATIONS?

There are two ways in which behavioral scientists have tried to answer this question.

Information about Job Openings

Labor economists and industrial relations specialists have studied the information workers have about job openings and the sources used to obtain the information. The primary concern of these two groups has been to

---

[1] The motives behind this type of recruiter strategy, called here the *traditional method,* are discussed later in this chapter and are contrasted with *realistic recruitment.*

assess the degree of "economic rationality" characteristic of outsider individuals trying to learn about organizations. In contrast to this, psychologists have been concerned with what people know about the nature of the organization itself. These differences in orientation are typical of the two disciplines. Economists tend to be concerned with the search process for job openings whereas psychologists tend to focus on the expectations of outsider individuals and their reactions to the organizational climates as newcomers.

The economics and industrial relations literature on how workers find job openings has been reviewed twice (Parnes 1954 and 1970). In the first review, the author concluded that *informal* sources were used much more frequently than formal sources. This meant that workers found out about job openings via word of mouth through friends and relatives in about 80 percent of the cases. This conclusion was based on Parnes's interpretation of six studies which included ten groups of workers on 16 different jobs (Heneman, Fox, and Yoder 1948; Kerr 1942; Myers and MacLaurin 1943; Myers and Schultz 1951; Reynolds 1951; and de Schweinitz 1932). Besides using informal sources, workers were also not considered completely rational (in the sense of obtaining full labor-market information) because they made job choice decisions based on certain minimum standards. If an opening came along that met a worker's personal standards, it was usually taken. Classical economic theory, in contrast, holds that workers should have continued to search for alternative job openings in the hope of finding one that would be a perfect match, not just one that was minimally satisfactory.

In the updated review (Parnes 1970) a different picture emerged due to the addition of several newer studies. In the more recent review it was concluded that the behavior of white-collar workers differs considerably from the behavior of blue-collar workers. In particular, white-collar workers fit more closely the image of economic rationality because they tend to obtain much more information about job openings than do blue-collar workers. (See Foltman 1968; Rees 1966; and Sheppard and Belitsky 1966.) Rather than relying on informal sources about 80 percent of the time, white-collar workers obtain job openings information from formal sources about 50 percent of the time.

Information about Organizations Themselves

Based on the earlier discussion of the organizational entry Matching Model (Fig. 1.1), and the conflicts occurring during entry (Table 1.3), it should be quite clear at this point that individuals need complete and valid information to make effective organizational choices for themselves. This raises the issue of how much the typical "outsider" job candidate knows in comparison to more experienced "insider" members of organizations. Research on this issue has been conducted in business, education, and the armed services, and is reviewed next.

The most comprehensive, and longest in duration, of the studies in business organizations was conducted at the American Telephone and Telegraph (AT&T) company (Bray, Campbell, and Grant 1974). This study, known as the Management Progress Study, includes a wealth of data, and will be referred to later in Chapter 5 in which AT&T's selection procedures are discussed. A total of 274 college recruits, who were hired in the summers of 1956, 1957, 1959, and 1960, were assessed thoroughly by a team of professional industrial psychologists at the time of hiring. For the first eight years, their job performance, promotions, and job attitudes were monitored by the personnel research unit of AT&T. After eight years, the group had shrunk to 167, which formed the nucleus of the study, since complete data were available on each of them.

The first indication of unrealistic expectations held by these recruits came in the analysis of two sets of data: (1) what the recruits *wanted* in a job, and (2) what they *expected* to find at AT&T. The analysis of these two responses showed that the recruits expected to find jobs almost exactly like the ones they desired (the correlation between expectations and desires was .87). This was interpreted as completely unrealistic because it is a good example of how one's *desires* can influence one's *expectations*.

When attitudes toward AT&T were measured, there was a steady downward trend year after year. Clearly, the new recruits did not find the reality of organizational life to be quite as expected. Figure 2.2 shows this trend. It is clear from this that attitudes fell from high, positive levels initially to lower levels over the first eight years and that dropoff occurred for all employees, both high and low job performers. (The definition of successful performance was whether or not the employee had reached the third level of management, called middle management, by the eighth year with AT&T. Of the 167 who were in the full eight-year study, about 60 made it to middle management.)

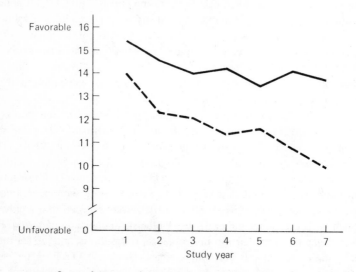

Fig. 2.2 *Attitudes at work for AT&T managers. (From D. W. Bray, R. J. Campbell, and D. L. Grant, 1974,* Formative Years in Business, *p. 158. Copyright © 1974 by John Wiley & Sons, Inc. Reprinted by permission of John Wiley & Sons, Inc.)*

The Ford Motor Company also tried to assess why some managers stayed and others left (Dunnette, Arvey, and Banas 1973). From a total group of more than 1,000, they divided the employees into Stayers (525) and Terminators (495), based on whether or not the person stayed or left within the first four years of employment.

For the Stayer group, the researchers found that four of the five *most important* job characteristics also had the largest *discrepancies* between expectations and the employee's present experiences on the job. When the discrepancies were calculated for the *first* jobs held, three of the five most important characteristics were among those with the largest discrepancies between expectations and reality. Figure 2.3 shows these results.

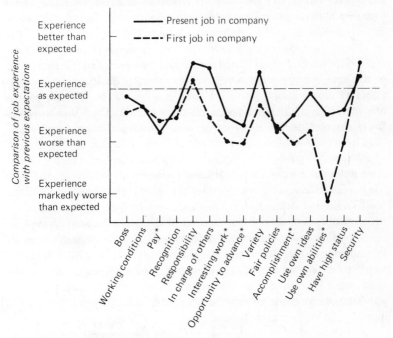

*Job features stated most important by college graduates

Fig. 2.3 *Discrepancies between job expectations and job experiences both for first jobs and later jobs at the Ford Motor Company. (From M. D. Dunnette, R. D. Arvey, and P. A. Banas, 1973, Why do they leave? Personnel 50 (3): 32. Reprinted by permission of the publisher. Copyright © 1973 by AMACOM, a division of American Management Associations. All rights reserved.)*

The fact that the largest discrepancies found were for those job facets rated as most important had very significant implications for the management at Ford. It is also important to note that the greatest *dis*confirmation of expectations by reality occurs for one's *first* job, rather than for later jobs held within the company. This may be due to the fact that people are able to switch to jobs that are closer to expectations. A second reason why there was a smaller discrepancy for subsequent job choices is the fact that insider experience teaches individuals what to expect. Of the important job characteristics, pay level was the closest to what was expected. This is probably because pay is easy to measure and can therefore be checked on by job candidates, as found earlier by Wanous (1972b).

Finally, a study of newly hired telephone operators (Wanous 1976) also showed the decline from inflated to lower (i.e., more realistic) expectations. In this case, the operators were asked to complete questionnaires at three stages of organizational entry (1) prior to entry, (2) as newcomers, after one month, and (3) as insiders, after three months. There was an across-the-board decline for all types of organizational climate expectations, ". . . from naive expectations to realistic beliefs" (Wanous 1976, p. 27).

Where do employees in business get such inflated expectations? There is no definitive answer to this, although research on MBA graduates from the Harvard Business School identifies one source—recruiters from business itself (Ward and Athos 1972). This study, conducted by two professors at that school, examined the expectations of 378 students. Student expectations for a particular company were compared with the descriptions of the same company given by recruiters. There were very few differences between these two sources of data across 14 different types of expectations about work. The correlation between the expectations of students and the job descriptions given by recruiters was .48, indicating the influence of recruiters on student expectations.

Based on what is now known, the same phenomenon of inflated expectations held by outsiders to business organizations occurs both in educational organizations and in the armed services. Research on those types of organizations is discussed next.

Ever since the advent of the all-volunteer armed services, there has been increased interest on the part of the various services to study problems of recruitment, selection, and reenlistment of volunteers. The armed forces now face many of the same problems as private industry in this regard. [See Hoiberg and Berry (1978) for a study of the Navy.]

A variety of studies have been done to identify the "market image" of various armed services, as an aid in the recruitment process. A recent summary of all this research serves as a good example of what is happening there (Wiskoff 1977). Some conclusions drawn by the author include:

1. Regardless of the country (Australia, Canada, the United Kingdom, or

the United States), youth seem to hold similar attitudes about life in the armed services.

2. The expectations of preservice individuals are usually in error, and are usually inflated, but with a few important exceptions.

3. The exceptions to the general trend of inflated expectations are pay levels and the severity of basic training. Pay is better than expected and basic training is not as bad as feared.

4. Recruiters are the major source for creating expectations of those not already in the military service.

5. Intentions to remain in service decline the longer someone is in the service.

There are some striking similarities between these conclusions and what has already been described in business. For example, the significance of recruiters in the forming of initial expectations was also found in the study of Harvard Business School MBAs. The tendency for attitudes toward one's own organization to decline with increasing experience is identical to the tendency detected by the AT&T research. Finally, the fact that outsider expectations are usually inflated is consistent with the results of private industry, but there are exceptions in the military. (The major exception seems to be that basic training is not as bad as expected. See Chapter 6 for an account of how basic training socializes army recruits.)

Similar results can be found in educational organizations, too. The most detailed study done in schools was of three different graduate schools of business administration in New York City (Wanous 1976). The incoming MBA candidates filled out questionnaires at three points during entry into these schools: (1) as outsiders in the summer before entry, (2) as newcomers during the fall of the first year, and (3) as insiders at the end of the spring term.

The 15 specific questions asked these individuals could be collapsed into two broad categories: (1) intrinsic to the process of education, e.g., excellent teaching, competition for grades, practical skills being taught, chances for personal growth, etc., and (2) extrinsic to the learning process, e.g., reasonable tuition, location of school, getting credit for previous work, and an attractive atmosphere, etc. Of these two categories, there was a clear decline for the intrinsic, not extrinsic, factors from naive (i.e., inflated) levels to more realistic (i.e., lower) levels. In contrast, the students seemed to have fairly realistic expectations about concrete, practical matters. The best explanation for these results is that the intrinsic factors were too abstract for students to obtain solid information. On the other hand, a factor such as tuition could be accurately assessed by outsiders who have not actually been inside the organization.

CONSEQUENCE OF UNREALISTIC EXPECTATIONS: LOW SATISFACTION

It is quite reasonable to predict that newcomers to organizations will be disappointed when they realize that many of their expectations will not be met. This is because a basic principle of psychology is that *satisfaction* is the result of some type of *comparison process,* although the exact nature of "What is compared to what?" has not been established by research (Wanous and Lawler 1972). Thus it is reasonable to expect *decreasing* satisfaction with one's organizational choice when that choice was made on the basis of inflated expectations. Several research studies have confirmed that this is exactly what happens.

Five studies of newcomers to organizations have examined satisfaction with various aspects of the organization. Once again the AT&T study (Bray et al. 1974) contains significant data gathered on a yearly basis for the first eight years with that company. The AT&T researchers divided their questions into those concerning *personal* versus *job* satisfaction. For *personal* satisfaction, there was a decline up to the third year, a slight rise for the next two years, and then a slight falling. The difference between the first and last measurements was not statistically significant, although personal satisfaction was lower at the end of the study. The group of managers was split into those who made it to third level (i.e., middle) management, and those who did not. As might be expected, there were few initial differences. After the third year these two groups became quite different in terms of personal satisfaction. The successful group's average continued to rise from the third year on, whereas the unsuccessful group showed only a slight rise after year three and then a decline.

The *job* satisfaction trend for the AT&T managers was different from the personal satisfaction trend. Instead of dropping the first three years, there was a slight rise. This, however, was followed by a steady decline so that final level of job satisfaction was significantly lower than the initial level. In contrast to personal staisfaction, there were few differences in job satisfaction between successful and less successful groups.

A study done at Sears (Smith, Roberts, and Hulin 1976) gathered job satisfaction data from over 98,000 blue- and white-collar employees at 132 branches located throughout the United States. Data were collapsed into three time periods extending over a ten-year span of time (1963–1969, 1967–1970, 1971–1972). A total of seven areas were measured (supervision, financial rewards, career future, kind of work, etc).

On an overall basis the Sears data show a downward trend for five of the seven areas of job satisfaction. One area did not change (amount of work done), and one area dropped and then rose (financial rewards). To try to isolate trends for the newly entered employees, those with less than one year's tenure in the 1967–1970 group were compared with those with one to five years of service in the 1971–1972 group. There was a decline for five of the seven areas (supervision, amount of work done, co-workers, physical surroundings, and career future). Kind of work done and financial rewards both increased.

The AT&T and Sears studies show a general decrease in satisfaction with increasing tenure in an organization. In both cases, however, no data were gathered *prior* to entry into these two companies. Three other studies described below did obtain both preentry and postentry data. The most ambitious of these three traced the attitudes of college accounting majors as they took jobs after graduation (Lawler, Kuleck, Rhode, and Sorenson 1975). An initial group of 711 provided data prior to making an organizational choice; 431 continued in the study by responding to the post-choice questionnaire; 197 provided data after one year on the job. The attractiveness of the accounting firm chosen for one's first job increased immediately after making the choice, but fell in the one-year follow-up. It should be remembered that the immediate post-choice data were gathered *prior* to entry.

A smaller study of Carnegie–Mellon graduates found the same decreasing satisfaction phenomenon (Vroom 1966; Vroom and Deci 1971). After one year on the job, 31 of 39 subjects (80 percent) saw their chosen company as less attractive than they saw it initially. After 3.5 years, 12 subjects had changed jobs and were more satisfied than those who remained in their original organizations.

Finally, a study of college graduates entering MBA programs (Wanous 1975c) in three New York City graduate schools of business administration also found the decreasing satisfaction trend from preentry to postentry. The attractiveness of each school steadily dropped from prior to entry, to two months after entry, to eight months after entry.

SOURCES USED BY ORGANIZATIONS TO FIND NEWCOMERS

The importance of where one obtains newcomers can be seen in the recent experience of the United States Military Academy at West Point in the recruitment of women cadets (Feron 1977). On an overall basis, 119 women were admitted in the fall of 1976, and 89 remained after the first year (a dropout rate 5 percent higher than for the men). However, a closer look at where these women came from showed that those women who came directly from high school were more likely to stay than were those who transferred from another college. To help in the 1977 recruiting, copies of newspaper articles were photocopied and sent to all applicants in an effort to reduce the reality shock upon arrival at West Point. (In the next chapter, we will also see that West Point had earlier experimented with similar "realistic previews" for male cadets.)

There have been many more studies listing the types of sources used to recruit newcomers than there have been of how *effective* each of these sources is. The important question here is not to identify the sources used (e.g., Malm 1954), but to go further and relate long-term employee success to the sources from which the good employees came. Unfortunately, there have only been four such studies (Decker and Cornelius 1979; Gannon 1971; LIMRA 1962; Reid 1972).

One study examined the sources from which a New York bank hired personnel, and related the source of hiring to subsequent turnover rates for the first year at work. Table 2.1 shows these results. The difference between a "major" and nonmajor hiring agency was simply that the "major" one was under a contract with the bank to provide new recruits.

A study by LIMRA (Life Insurance Marketing Research Association) of 38,000 individuals looked at how well recruits from different sources did on the selection test for a life insurance agent. Sources of applicants who did *poorly* were (1) newspaper ads, (2) college or business school referrals, and (3) employment agency referrals. Recruits from the following sources did quite well on the selection test: (1) self-initiated contact by the applicant, or (2) referred by another person at an insurance agency.

TABLE 2.1

Source of referral and quit rate

SOURCE	NUMBER HIRED	NUMBER WHO QUIT	PERCENTAGE OF THOSE WHO QUIT	
Reemployed	253	54	21.3	Good sources
Referred by high school workshop	602	131	21.8	
Referred by present employees	2,320	615	26.5	
Walk-ins	1,212	349	28.8	
Hiring agencies (except "major")	637	241	37.8	Poor sources
Newspaper ads	512	202	39.4	
Major hiring agency	854	342	40.0	
Totals	6,390	1,934	30.3	

Source: M. J. Gannon, 1971. Sources of referral and employee turnover. *Journal of Applied Psychology* 55: 227. Copyright 1971 by the American Psychological Association. Reprinted by permission.

A study of 279 British trades workers hired in 1966–1968 found job survival to be greatest when employee referrals and job posting were sources. When new hires came from newspaper ads or employment agencies, job survival was less. More recently, a study of 1,753 insurance agents, 514 bank employees, and 199 professional abstractors found a similar trend (Decker and Cornelius 1979). Employee referral was the best source for obtaining long-tenure employees in all three samples. Newspaper advertising was the worst source in two of the three samples, as was an employment agency source.

There appears to be a clear trend running through these studies. Sources that provide job candidates with the most realistic picture of a job situation are those that provide the employer with longer tenure employees. Examples of these sources are referral by a present employee, or being reemployed by the same company. Those sources, e.g., employment agencies or newspaper ads, from which job candidates get less information (and probably only positive information) yield new employees with much lower job survival rates.

Sources of effective new organization members are of crucial importance to organizations—so important, in fact, that most businesses do not publish the results of their own surveys. Such information is considered a business secret because it can give a company a competitive edge over its rivals. The personnel costs from turnover have already been documented in Chapter 1, so it's not hard to understand why this is a fact.

The remainder of this chapter is an extended discussion of different philosophies, or strategies, of how to recruit newcomers to organizations. The nature of the *traditional* versus *realistic* philosophies is explained. This section is the prelude to Chapter 3 that goes into greater detail on the realistic recruitment method.

CONTRASTING PHILOSOPHIES OF RECRUITMENT

Earlier in this chapter, a model (Fig. 2.1) was shown that outlined a variety of conflicts that occur during "mutual selection and attraction processes" (Porter, Lawler, and Hackman 1975). One of the four conflicts shown concerns organizational recruitment philosophy. Those actions taken by organizations to *attract* newcomers are often at odds with the effective *selection* and *retention* of them.

In this section of the chapter, the roots of this "attraction and selection conflict" are explored. However, it will become clear that *this conflict need not occur*. The conflict is, however, quite real and serious for those organizations that recruit newcomers according to the traditional philosophy (Wanous 1975a). Those organizations that have used the realistic recruitment philosophy do *not* experience the conflict between effective attraction on the one hand, and effective selection and retention, on the other.

Let's now explore exactly what is meant by traditional and realistic recruitment strategies, or philosophies. The next chapter will focus specifically on the methods of realistic recruitment, the results from organizations which have used it, and those practical and theoretical problems that still need to be worked out by researchers and practicing managers.

Traditional Recruitment

The traditional philosophy of recruitment can be best summarized as the practice of "selling" the organization to outsiders. Specifically, this selling of the organization involves two actions: (1) only positive characteristics are communicated to outsiders rather than those things insiders find dissatisfying about the organization, and (2) those features that are advertised may be distorted to make them seem even more positive. The former practice is called presenting *deficient* information (i.e., omitting the negative) to outsiders, and is quite typical of traditional recruitment. The latter practice injects *bias* into that information given out during recruitment, and is much less typical.

Therefore, traditional recruitment is designed to attract as many candidates as possible. Since this is in conflict with the organization's ability to retain newcomers, it is important that the reasons behind sticking to such a policy be analyzed. There are at least four reasons that have been used to justify the traditional approach: (1) the need for a favorable selection ratio, (2) the desire to retain control or initiative in the entry process, (3) the problems of measuring needs versus abilities, and (4) the concern with job performance rather than job satisfaction.

Need for favorable selection ratio

The selection ratio of an organization is the proportion of job candidates who are hired. For example, if 100 people apply and 10 are actually hired, the selection ratio is .10 (i.e., $10 \div 100$), or 10 percent of those who applied. The maximum selection ratio that can occur is 1.00, a situation in which every applicant is accepted and not one is turned away.

Organizations that have personnel departments that do the selecting of newcomers must justify their own budget. A company with a selection ratio of 1.00 has very little need to spend much money on a personnel department to do employee selection. On the other hand, one with a selection ratio of .10 definitely needs to budget money for a personnel department because it must find a way of rejecting 90 percent of the applicants. In this latter case, it is much easier to justify the personnel budget. Therefore, in organizational terms, a "favorable" selection ratio is one that is *low,* i.e., a small proportion of those who apply are actually hired.

One way to make the selection ratio favorable is to use the traditional strategy of selling the organization. By attracting a relatively large pool of applicants, the selection ratio can be lowered. In this way, the personnel department is quite active because it processes more applicants and looks like a good budgetary investment because a larger proportion of applicants needs to be rejected.

(2) *Desire to retain initiative and control within the organization*

The more a company or school sells itself, the more attractive it will appear to outsiders, and the more applicants it will receive. When this occurs, the selection ratio drops to a more favorable level, as discussed above. At the same time, however, the degree of control over the influx of newcomers is increased from the organization's perspective. The greater the percentage of "no admittance" decisions, the greater the control the organization has over the input of newcomers. This is an easy way to reduce the risk involved in bringing any newcomer on board.

(3) *Matching abilities, rather than needs, to the organization is the top concern*

In the first chapter, the Matching Model (Fig. 1.1) was shown. The upper portion of that model concerned the match between an individual's abilities (or future potential) and those abilities required by the organization.

Although this was only one of the two matchings, most organizations have put their strongest efforts toward the ability and job requirements match, rather than toward the individual needs and organizational climates match. One reason for this difference in emphasis is that tests of human abilities are not as easy to fake as those that try to measure human needs. To obtain accurate data on abilities, the organization needs a valid assessment procedure. (See Chapter 5 for further discussion.) However, to obtain accurate information about human needs, *both* a valid measurement procedure and the willingness of the individual to provide honest answers are needed.[2] A second reason for this is that the impact of an ability and job requirements mismatch falls most directly on job performance, and this is *assumed* to be *more* costly than the low job satisfaction or organizational commitment resulting from the mismatch between individual needs and organizational climates.

This overemphasis on matching abilities to job requirements is another reason for the traditional selling of the organization to potential new members. This is because there is the obvious desire to obtain the *best* possible (meaning most able) newcomers. Since this is the major concern,

---

[2] In research on consumer preferences for certain products, various methods for obtaining valid data have been developed which do *not* depend on the honest cooperation of individuals. These have involved various physiological measures such as how the pupils of one's eyes expand when viewing certain products. In organizational research, no such measures have been tried.

the best way to do so is to *attract* as many applicants as possible and then *select* those who demonstrate the greatest competence.

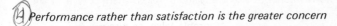

Performance rather than satisfaction is the greater concern

There are at least two reasons why job performance, rather than job satisfaction, is of greater concern to most organizations. The first is that the dollar costs of poor performance are felt immediately by the organization and are easier to calculate than are those associated with low job satisfaction. The second reason is that the dollar consequences of negative job attitudes have not been as easy to document in the past as they are today. Job satisfaction is related to many other outcomes at work, such as quitting, absenteeism, accidents, and mental illness (and sometimes, but not consistently, to job performance, too), but satisfaction is not strongly connected to any of these outcomes. The strongest link with job satisfaction appears to be employee turnover (Porter and Steers 1973), rather than absenteeism (Nicholson, Brown, and Chadwick-Jones 1976).

Realistic Recruitment

Rather than "selling" the organization, realistic recruitment presents outsiders with *all pertinent* information *without distortion*. In the remainder of this chapter, the rationale for realistic recruitment is presented. In the following chapter, the practical issues of how to do it, the research results from those organizations that have used realism, and the theoretical issues concerning realistic recruitment are presented. The best way to understand how this philosophy differs from the traditional approach is to contrast the reasons for using realism with those used to justify the traditional method.

The need for a favorable selection ratio is a myopic view

There is nothing logically wrong with an organization wanting to become "more selective," i.e., to have a low selection ratio, because it does provide powerful justification for the budgetary dollars allocated to the personnel selection process. The problem with using the selection ratio as the rationale for traditional recruitment is that it is too narrow a view of the entire organizational entry process. It is narrow in the sense that it tends to ignore what happens to newcomers *after* they are inside the new organization. A broader perspective includes not only attracting and selecting competent newcomers but also managing to *retain* them as well. It will be seen in the next chapter that the realistic strategy results in less turnover than the traditional method without any sacrifice in job performance.

(2) *Organizational control of its own boundary is being decreased by new laws concerning personnel selection*

A reason for the former popularity of traditional recruitment was that it tended to retain initiative and control inside the organization. Although we have seen that organizational entry is a two-sided choice process (Fig. 2.1), traditional recruitment does tend to put the final choice initiative more in the control of the organization than of the individual. This occurs for two reasons. First, the desire of individuals to join the organization is artificially increased by the selling approach so that relatively few persons are discouraged from considering the organization. Second, by having a low (highly selective) selection ratio, the organization retains control over who gets in and who does not.

With the Civil Rights Act of 1964 and the subsequent guidelines for selection issued by the Equal Employment Opportunity Commission (EEOC) and by the Office of Federal Contract Compliance (OFCC), many organizations, especially business organizations, have found it harder and harder to make selection decisions based on nonjob-related factors. Today, job performance is considered as virtually the only valid basis for selecting new employees. If a particular method of selection cannot be related to subsequent job performance, it is illegal. The "burden of proof" now rests on the shoulders of the organization making selection decisions, rather than on the shoulders of the individual going through this process (Arvey 1979).

The net effect has been to decrease the degree of arbitrary control an organization can exert over the input of newcomers. Simultaneously, the importance of the *self*-selection decisions of individuals (see Chapter 4 on Organizational Choice) has increased. Although these self-selection decisions are not directly controllable, they *are* capable of being influenced by the organization.

The issue today is how an organization wants to influence the individual's choice of an organization. All types of organizations are going to have an increasing stake in the accuracy of these choices.

Matching needs to the organizational climate can be done

A reason for not trying to match needs to climate was the difficulty encountered in trying to do so. Since self-report measures of what individuals
want from a job can be easily faked, those who use traditional recruitment
can justify their choice in these terms. There is, however, another way in
which needs may be more closely aligned with the organization's climate,
and it does not have the faking problem. Simply put, realistic recruitment
presents the individual with a large amount of valid data about an organization. The more and better the information, the better each person can
decide whether or not to try to join. In other words, matching individual
needs and organizational climates can be achieved via the organizational
choices made by individuals themselves.

The importance of job satisfaction is increasing

Within just the last few years, researchers have been able to estimate the
dollar value of various employee behaviors and then relate these behaviors
to job satisfaction. The end result has been the ability to demonstrate how
changes in satisfaction cause changes in job behavior, and how much these
changes can either cost a company money or be a cost savings for a company. Let's see how this has been done in practice by examining what happened when two researchers studied 160 tellers in a midwestern bank
(Mirvis and Lawler 1977).

Three types of on-the-job behavior were examined for their costs to
the organization and for how closely they were influenced by job satisfaction: (1) absenteeism, (2) turnover, and (3) shortages. Table 2.2
shows both the variable costs and the total costs of both absenteeism and
turnover.

In the case of absenteeism, there are five separate types of costs in-
curred by the bank. The first of these, salary, is a variable cost because this
bank did not pay for days absent. The remaining four cost sources are not
under the immediate control of the bank. The "unabsorbed overhead rate"
refers to all expenses (e.g., lights, rent, staff functions, etc.) that are allocated to the department for a particular level of staff. The cost figures
for turnover refer to voluntary quits, rather than involuntary termination.
The final job behavior, teller shortages, refers to the cost of dealing with
discrepancies between how much cash is actually in a teller's drawer at the
end of the day compared with how much should be there. At this bank,

TABLE 2.2

Cost per incident of absenteeism and turnover

VARIABLE	COST (IN DOLLARS)
Absenteeism	
Absent employee	
Salary	23.04
Benefits	6.40
Replacement employee:	
Training and staff time	2.13
Unabsorbed burden	15.71
Lost profit contribution	19.17
Total variable cost	23.04
Total cost	66.45
Turnover	
Replacement acquisition	
Direct hiring costs	293.95
Other hiring costs	185.55
Replacement training	
Preassignment	758.84
Learning curve	212.98
Unabsorbed burden	682.44
Lost profit contribution	388.27
Total variable cost	293.95
Total cost	2,522.03

Source: P. H. Mirvis and E. E. Lawler, III, 1977. Measuring the financial impact of employee attitudes. *Journal of Applied Psychology* **62**: 4, Table 2. Copyright 1977 by the American Psychological Association. Reprinted by permission.

there was an average of 3.07 teller shortages per employee per month, for a total of $25.27 per employee each month, or a bankwide total of $4,043.20 every month. There was an average of 37.76 days absent per month for a bankwide cost of $2,509.15. Finally, there was an average of 9.28 persons quitting per month, for a bankwide cost of $23,404.44. All costs together totaled $29,956.79 each month of the year, or $359,481.48 *each year*!

Low job satisfaction did not account for all of these costs, of course, but it was causing some of them. Job satisfaction was measured by asking the tellers to answer six questions about their jobs. Each question could be rated from 1 (lowest) to 7 (highest), and the average level of satisfaction across all six items was 4.8 for the bank. The researchers then estimated that if this level of job satisfaction could be increased up to 5.5, the bank would realize a cost savings of $1,472 per month, or $17,664 per year. On the other hand, if satisfaction were to decrease in the future by an equal amount (to 4.1), $17,664 would be *added* to the bank's operating costs for the year. [See Mirvis and Lawler (1977) for details.]

PURPOSE AND THEORY OF REALISTIC RECRUITMENT

With everything that's been said up to now, it should be clear that realistic recruitment is designed to increase job satisfaction. Thus realism reduces subsequent unnecessary turnover caused by the disappointment of initial expectations inflated by traditional recruitment. Figure 2.4 shows how this worked at the Southern New England Telephone Company where realistic recruitment was used for hiring telephone operators (Wanous 1973, 1975a, b). It can be seen from Fig. 2.4 that the highly inflated expectations, caused by traditional recruitment, represent an important source of initial job dissatisfaction since they are much higher than the level actually found on the job.

Another way to describe the effect of lowering job expectations *before* entering the organization is to call realistic recruitment a "vaccination" (McGuire 1964) against the negative aspects of real organizational life. The medical concept of a vaccination is to inject a person with a weak dosage of the actual organisms that cause a particular disease, for example, smallpox virus. The purpose is to help the human body develop its own resistance to the virus and thus *prevent* the disease. The vaccination will *not* cure someone who has already contracted the disease.

Realistic recruitment operates in much the same way as a medical vaccination works because job candidates are given a small dose of organizational reality during the recruitment stage in an attempt to lower initial expectations. (Earlier it was shown that inflated expectations are quite typical for outsiders in the process of organizational entry.) In a manner similar to medical vaccination, realism is ineffective *after* a person is already inside a new organization, since actual job experience provides an ample source of realism.

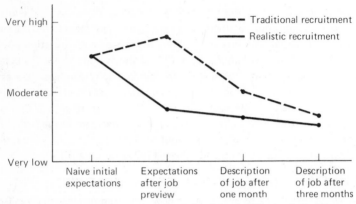

Fig. 2.4 *How attitudes about work change. (From J. P. Wanous, 1975b, Tell it like it is at realistic job previews.* Personnel *52(4): 58.*

Besides the "vaccination effect," there are at least two other ways that realism in recruitment can increase initial job satisfaction and thereby reduce turnover of new employees. One is the "self-selection, matching effect" and the other is the "personal commitment" effect. The relationships among all three of these are shown in Fig. 2.5.

Besides the vaccination of initial job expectations, turnover can be reduced by a better matching of individual needs and organizational climates. This relationship is a straightforward derivative from the Matching Model (Fig. 1.1). Since people strive to be satisfied, they tend to choose organizations that they believe will lead to personal satisfaction. (See Chapter 4 for the research results on this point.) The better the information job candidates possess, the more effective their own organizational choice can be.

Finally, when individuals believe that *they* made a decision without coercion or strong inducements from others, they tend to be much more *committed* to the decision (Bem 1970). In situations of coercion or strong external inducements, individuals may comply, but typically do not feel the internal commitment that comes from making their own choices. This is why the research literature on "participation in decision making" has consistently shown that people accept decisions that they have had a hand in making (Vroom 1970).

The last thing to note here is that these three mechanisms are interlocked. In order for the vaccination effect to occur, the organization must

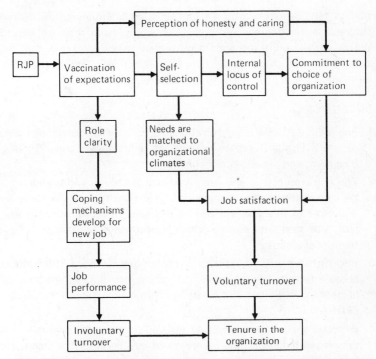

Fig. 2.5 *Psychological effects of the realistic job preview (RJP). (From J. P. Wanous, 1978, Realisitic job previews: Can a procedure to reduce turnover also influence the relationship between abilities and performance? Personnel Psychology 31: 251. Reprinted by permission.)*

use realistic recruitment. In order for the self-selection matching effect to occur, the vaccination effect must have happened. If expectations have not been "set" at realistic levels, then effective needs–climates matching cannot follow. Finally, the personal commitment effect is contingent upon the individual making an organizational choice. In some cases people get only one job offer, so there is little chance to make a meaningful choice.

In some situations the vaccination effect can occur alone without either of the other two. However, the self-selection matching effect cannot occur without a prior vaccination. Also, the commitment mechanism is contingent upon a prior vaccination. This interdependency among the psychological mechanisms of realistic recruitment has caused difficult problems for researchers who are interested in determining how realism affects job satisfaction and turnover. On the other hand, it has not caused problems for personnel managers because their major concern is with the *degree* of turnover reduction due to realism, rather than with the psychological theory of *how* realism acts to reduce turnover.

CONCLUSIONS

1. The joining process of organizational entry is a *dual* matching process between (1) human capabilities and job requirements, and (2) individual needs and organizational climates.

2. The entry process is also one of *mutual* attraction and selection between individuals and organizations. Traditionally speaking, there are a number of inherent conflicts in this view of organizational entry, but these need not occur if realistic recruitment is used instead of the traditional approach.

3. Recruits have inflated expectations about organizations. This happens because recruits cannot easily disentangle their hopes from their expectations. Recruiters also create unrealistic expectations for job candidates.

4. Expectations are most seriously inflated for the most important job factors, with the possible exception of pay because it is a concrete factor. Pay can be checked by an outsider.

5. Favorable attitudes toward organizations decrease the longer newcomers remain in them—as long as eight or ten years in AT&T or Sears.

6. The best "sources of referral" for new employees are those from which the recruit will be likely to already have realistic expectations, such as former employees being reemployed or those referred by present employees. Employment agencies and newspaper ads are the worst sources.

7. The logical case for realistic recruitment seems more compelling than the case for continued use of traditional methods.

8. The psychology of how realism in recruitment acts to increase job satisfaction and reduce turnover is intricate. The "vaccination" of expectations seems to be the cornerstone of this psychological process. A more effective matching between person and organization is also a likely explanation, as is increased commitment to an organizational choice made without much external pressure or coercion.

Realistic Recruitment

3

The focus of this chapter is narrower than that of Chapter 2. One specific aspect of organizational recruitment, the use of *realism,* is examined in four ways: (1) how to diagnose the possible need for realistic recruitment, (2) how to develop and provide a realistic job preview during recruitment, (3) an evaluation of the effects of realistic recruitment, and (4) guidelines for the use of realistic recruitment. This chapter is addressed to organizations who recruit newcomers rather than to the newcomers themselves. It is designed as a guide for those involved in personnel recruitment for various types of organizations.

DIAGNOSIS OF THE NEED FOR REALISTIC RECRUITMENT

Since realistic recruitment is a radical departure from typical organizational practice, it is necessary to determine whether or not organizational conditions warrant the installation of it as part of the personnel function. The Matching Model (Fig. 1.1) clearly shows that job satisfaction, organizational commitment, and *voluntary* turnover are the most fertile areas to search for signs of ineffective recruitment. Thus these areas must be monitored during the entry of newcomers. In addition to gathering these data, the organization should also gather information on a variety of specific expectations held by outsiders in order to determine whether or not these expectations are confirmed after entry. Data on *expectation* confirmation (*or disconfirmation*) are important because they can pinpoint areas in need of effort to provide realistic information to recruits.

Ineffective recruitment may also have an effect on job performance and, consequently, on *in*voluntary turnover. In theory, the *selection* function (see Chapter 5) is designed to screen out those with inappropriate abilities who may be recruited into an organization. Since selection procedures are far from foolproof, there is no doubt that ineffective recruitment can sometimes create unnecessary involuntary turnover.

While recruitment practices may affect job performance and involuntary turnover, the main impact of recruitment is on "lower" part of the Matching Model (job satisfaction, organizational commitment, and voluntary turnover). Actually, the degree to which recruitment practices may affect job performance and involuntary turnover is governed by the *selection ratio* for a particular job. For example, when only a few candidates apply for a position in relation to the number of openings, it is difficult for the selection procedures to screen out inappropriate candidates. Thus recruitment practices assume a larger role in influencing all components of the Matching Model when the selection ratio is high. On the other hand, if the ratio is *low* (a small percentage of applicants is actually hired), the impact of recruitment is limited mostly to the matching of human needs with the various organizational climates. In the remainder of this chapter, the discussion focuses on the direct effects of ineffective recruitment (satisfaction, commitment, and voluntary turnover) rather than on the indirect effects (performance and involuntary turnover).

To monitor an organization for the major symptoms of ineffective recruitment, three types of data from newcomers must be collected: (1) the degree to which expectations are confirmed by experience, (2) satisfaction and commitment, and (3) voluntary turnover rates. Expectation confirmation refers to the comparison of *two* pieces of data: (1) *expectations* reported by *outsiders* to an organization, and (2) *descriptions* of the same job and organization *after* the individual has entered the new organization. In contrast, job satisfaction is how one feels about the job itself, and commitment refers to one's attachment to the organization. Organizations need to be able to identify those *specific areas* in which outsiders have inflated expectations, so it is very important that expectation confirmation be measured. Just asking newcomers how satisfied or committed they are does not provide this detailed information.

Measuring voluntary turnover is actually quite complicated. First of all, a job *survival* rate should be calculated for newcomers in specific jobs. This can be calculated in several ways. One is to see how many newcomers are still employed after a certain amount of time has gone by, e.g., six months or a year. When newcomers enter as a group (rather than coming in smaller numbers, but in a steady "trickle"), it is possible to calculate the "half-life" of the group, that is, how long it takes for 50 percent of the group to leave the organization. Both of these methods are preferable to calculating turnover as a percentage of the total work force of an organization. This is because the total force contains too diverse a grouping.

After calculating job survival rates or the half-life of newcomers, separating voluntary from involuntary turnover is still very difficult. Voluntary turnover refers to the *individual's* decision to leave the organization. Quitting is the most common form, although people resign for other reasons, e.g., to accommodate a marriage partner. In contrast, involuntary turnover refers to actions initiated by the organization, e.g., dismissals, layoffs, retirements. The method of categorizing turnover is imperfect because it depends on the quality of information obtained. Sometimes individuals quit if they know they are going to be fired. Depending on which source was used for data (the employee or the organization), a different version of the situation might be obtained.

An important consideration in measuring turnover is to account for the possible effects of performance appraisal on the job survival of newcomers. In many organizations, there is a period in which newcomers are not subject to a job performance appraisal, e.g., students have either a quarter or a semester before course grades are final. In business the same thing can happen, e.g., new sales personnel at Xerox or IBM often hold a salaried position (during training) for about a year before going to a commission-on-sales method of payment. These companies have low turnover during this first year, but much higher turnover after the newcomers are put in the field. Similar results have been found with those who sell life insurance. Thus the onset of performance appraisal for newcomers can itself be a cause of turnover for three reasons. First, newcomers may be dismissed for poor performance. Second, newcomers discover for themselves that they are not really qualified to do the new job, and decide to leave. Third, they can find that the actual job duties are not sufficiently interesting, but this decision is not reached until after the initial training period is completed. The first of these is called involuntary turnover and the latter two are called voluntary.

Since the purpose of this diagnosis is to identify problems in recruitment, *not other organizational problems,* a general rule is that such measurements should be made right after entry and should continue regularly for at least several months. The longer newcomers are inside organizations, the *less* likely are their attitudes and behavior a result of entry, hence the need for early and continuous monitoring of newcomers.

Unfortunately, no detailed rules apply to exactly how this monitoring should be done. The situation is not entirely hopeless, however, since there are some general considerations that can be used in deciding when and how often to monitor the symptoms of ineffective recruitment. One is to account for the difference between initial experiences during training and those experiences once one is actually on the job full time. Another is to account for the basic *type* of organization; e.g., the critical problem for the armed services is reenlistment, not early turnover. Similarly, in colleges one critical period occurs at the end of a term period and an even more critical period occurs at the end of the academic year. In some businesses, the critical period may last nine months to a year, whereas in others it may be much shorter—days or weeks.

A CASE STUDY OF DIAGNOSIS:
SOUTHERN NEW ENGLAND TELEPHONE (SNET)

At the outset, SNET did *not* have the diagnostic information on possible symptoms of ineffective recruitment. There were no satisfaction data on newcomers, and there was no monitoring of newcomers' perceptions to determine possible discrepancies between the expected and actual organizational climates. The turnover data did, however, indicate that there *might* be a recruitment problem among operators. The turnover rate for all operators, regardless of how long they were employed by SNET, was about 30 to 35 percent in 1971. However, when the turnover rate of operators who had been employed for six months or less was examined, it was found to be 150 percent on an annual basis.

Judging on these turnover data only, the company president felt something had to be done. Rather than trying to collect additional diagnostic data, the president decided the next step was to get a clearer picture of the operator's job.

The diagnosis of job and organizational conditions used three *methods*: interviews, questionnaires, and participant observation. Two *sources* were used: presently employed operators and their supervisors.

The overselling of the operator's job to recruits quickly emerged from the comparison of diagnostic data from experienced operators

ADMINISTRATIVE ASSISTANT

Here's your chance to enter the challenging and competitive world of publishing. You will be directly involved in the behind-the-scenes action for new best-sellers, college textbooks, and so forth.

The Administrative Assistant works directly with our editorial staff and our production department. Major job duties include handling correspondence with authors, arranging meetings, seeing that production schedules are met, and facilitating the smooth production of new books.

Wetson-Astley is located in Wrighting, Mass., a beautiful suburban area close to Boston. Starting salaries are among the highest in this industry.

Wetson-Astley is an equal opportunity employer.

Fig. 3.1 *Hypothetical example of unrealistic recruitment of secretarial help by a textbook publishing firm. This approach is similar to the approach used by SNET to recruit operators.*

with the printed material used to recruit newcomers. Similar results were found in the comparison of diagnostic data with interviews of company recruiters and the interviewers who made selection decisions. The discrepancy between what was told prospective operators and actual job conditions was understandable in the case of recruiters, since their job was defined by the company as that of providing a large pool of applicants. (This was a typical example of the selection ratio justification of traditional recruitment.) Those who made actual selection decisions also tended to oversell the job, but less so in comparison with the recruiters. If the company interviewers found a person who looked capable, they then went into the selling mode. Job candidates whose prospects seemed less bright did not receive as much attention.

Based on all this information, it was recommended that SNET experiment with realistic recruitment on a temporary basis in the hiring of new telephone operators to see if this change would increase the job survival of newcomers. Half of all newly hired operators were to be shown a short, job-preview film based on the realistic information obtained in the

Preexperimental	Experimental (realistic)	Experimental (traditional)
Receptionist	Receptionist	Receptionist
Initial interview	Initial interview	Initial interview
	Questionnaire 1	Questionnaire 1
Testing, medical questionnaire	Testing, medical questionnaire	Testing, medical questionnarie
Application blank	Application blank	Application blank
Selection interview	Selection interview	Selection interview
	Realistic film	Traditional film
	Questionnaire 2	Questionnaire 2
Job visit	Job visit	Job visit
Training	Training	Training
Work experience	Work—1 month: Questionnaire 3	Work—1 month: Questionnaire 3
	Work—3 months: Questionnaire 4	Work—3 months: Questionnaire 4

Fig. 3.2 *Design of realistic recruitment of telephone operators. (From J. P. Wanous, 1972a,* An Experimental Test of Job Attraction Theory in an Organizational Setting. *Unpublished doctoral dissertation. New Haven: Yale University.)*

diagnosis. The other half of those hired would be treated in pretty much the same (traditional) way as usual—except that they would see an AT&T produced film about the operator's job. This AT&T film had been previously used by SNET and other telephone companies in recruitment. It was designed to show the job in its most favorable terms; that is, the information in this film was correct (i.e., not biased), but it was *deficient* in that it showed, in the main, only positive characteristics.

The experiment was designed to be companywide, which meant that the six largest cities in Connecticut were sites for the study. At each site both films were available, but were alternated on a weekly basis to provide a random assignment of job previews to each job candidate processed by the employment office. The design of the study is outlined in Fig. 3.2.

REALISTIC RECRUITMENT IN PRACTICE

A variety of organizations (business, education, and the military) have all tried realistic recruitment in one form or another. The common element in all of these efforts is the attempt to increase the job survival of newcomers. The actual *means* used are, however, quite different. In this section several examples show the varieties of realistic recruitment. It should become clear that the use of realism is a *general approach* to recruitment, rather than a specific technique, and that it needs to be "tailor-made" for each individual organization.

Business Organizations

Studies of realistic recruitment can be found in a variety of businesses: SNET, operators; Bell Canada, operators; Prudential, life insurance agents; Life and Casualty of Tennessee, life insurance agents; Manhattan Industries, sewing machine operators; and checkout clerks in a supermarket chain. The procedures used for two of these are highlighted below as examples.

Telephone operators—SNET. Following the analysis of a telephone operator's job, an outline was prepared of the major positive and negative job characteristics, as reported by the operators and their supervisors. This outline served as the script for making a 15-minute film to be used as an alternative to the traditional recruiting film that the organization already had been using.

The company supplied six experienced operators whose answers to interview questions were videotaped for later editing. Figure 3.3 shows areas that were covered by both films, as well as those aspects unique to each one. After an individual had seen the realistic film, a pamphlet (see Fig. 3.4) was given out to reinforce the major points made in that film.

Overlap between Films

1. Customers can be quite unfriendly at times.
2. Work is fast paced.
3. Some operators receive satisfaction from helping out customers.
4. Action sequences of operators at work:
   a) emergency call,
   b) "wise guy" calling operator,
   c) credit card call,
   d) overseas call,
   e) directory assistance operators at work,
   f) "nasty" customer calling operator.
5. Dealing with others (customers, co-workers) is a large part of the job.

Nonoverlap Characteristics

Realistic film	*Traditional film*
1. Lack of variety.	1. Everyone seems happy at work.
2. Job is routine; may become boring.	2. Exciting work.
3. Close supervision; little freedom.	3. Important work.
4. Limited opportunity to make friends.	4. Challenging work.
5. Receive criticism for bad performance, but no praise when deserved.	
6. Challenging initially, but once learned is easy and not challenging.	

Fig. 3.3 *Job characteristics emphasized by each job preview film. (From J. P. Wanous, 1975b, Tell it like it is at realistic job previews, Personnel 53: 57. Copyright © 1975 by AMACOM, a division of American Management Associations. All rights reserved.)*

Life insurance agents—Prudential. The first published experimental study of realism was done at the Life and Casualty Insurance Company of Tennessee (Weitz 1956). Following this successful experiment, Prudential Insurance revised the booklet for its own study of life insurance agents (Youngberg 1963).

You have seen the film preview of the operator's job for two reasons:

1. We want you to know about the job before you decide if you want to be an operator.
2. If you become an operator, you will have a better idea of what to realistically expect on the job.

You are now given this folder which summarizes many important characteristics of the operator's job.

If you are a telephone operator, you can *realistically expect*:

- varied schedules—work on weekends, holidays, and at odd hours
- that regular attendance is required
- to help people complete calls or look up numbers for them
- that work will be closely supervised
- steady employment; full pay during training; good benefits and retirement
- routine work requiring strict attention to standard procedures
- that wage increases will be determined by job performance
- that accuracy and speed in work are required

Fig. 3.4 *Pamphlet used in conjunction with realistic job preview films.*

In both studies of agents a booklet was used, in contrast to the films used at SNET. Operators were shown a film only *after* a job offer was given, whereas the life insurance agents received booklets *before* a job offer was given. When an agent was sufficiently interested to sign up for the standardized selection test, the booklet was given out. (This difference in timing is important and will be discussed later in the last section of this chapter.)

Some samples from the Prudential booklet follow:

A Prudential representative finds that a high degree of personal recognition is available to him. And a successful Prudential Special Agent is recognized in his community as a professional man. But there are times when every Special Agent feels discouraged. A career as a Special Agent is not an easy one. It can mean many personal sacrifices; it can mean working four or more nights a week, in the beginning; it can mean postponing a special outing or an evening at home; it can mean having to take extra insurance courses to guarantee a better understanding of life insurance and the needs of clients.

A Special Agent is constantly faced with the challenge of finding the best solution to each new insurance problem he encounters. To find this solution, he must be willing and able to interpret a client's needs accurately; this often involves several interviews and considerable time. And, of course, time alone does not assure a sale. It is most important for a Special Agent to have the ability to answer objections and accept rejections. It is only through continuous practice that he learns to anticipate objections and answer them satisfactorily. But even the "correct approach" cannot guarantee a sale, and it often happens that a prospect's objections cannot be overcome. Each Agent must learn to accept the disappointments and frustrations which are an integral part of insurance selling. The ability to take rejections is of utmost importance for the insurance salesman.

The booklet also described the company's growth and support given to the agent by home office, agency, and manager. Before concluding with an emphasis on the "painstaking efforts" required, it pointed out a number of specific sources of conflict for every agent under the heading, "The Door to Success Does Not Open Easily."

The situations presented on these pages represent some of the problems which face every Agent. Thinking about what your reaction to them would be should help indicate whether or not you should pursue a life insurance sales career.

1. *An Agent spends several hours preparing a sound insurance program for a family . . . only to be turned down during the second interview.*

2. *An Agent completes the sale of a policy only to have the policyholder allow it to "lapse" by not paying a subsequent premium.*

3. *An Agent is sincerely interested in helping people plan their futures wisely, but, time after time, people say "No" to his recommendations.*

4. *An Agent makes the personal sacrifice of making a sales call on*

a stormy night only to find that the prospect has forgotten the
appointment and is not at home.

5. An Agent plans to attend an eagerly anticipated social event . . .
   but he has to postpone it because it is the only night a prospect
   can see him.

6. An Agent pays a call on a prospect to discuss insurance, only to
   be subjected to uncomplimentary . . . even though unwarranted
   . . . remarks about salesmen.

7. A conscientious Agent wants to qualify his prospects carefully
   and take time to visit policyholders whose insurance is about to
   lapse . . . but he knows that new prospects and new sales are also
   essential.

8. An Agent realizes that the Home Office tries to provide him with
   the best possible service, but he cannot help recalling the time an
   important case was lost because "the prospect cooled off" or
   "the competition moved in" while an application was being
   processed.

The Armed Forces

The United States Marine Corps developed an 80-minute videotape preview
of the training process that was shown to newly entered recruits. The content of the preview was obtained from extensive interviews with new recruits, those in the middle of training, and recent graduates of training.
Besides the recruits themselves, drill instructors and officers at several
levels were interviewed.

After the initial round of interviews, the experimenters had a reasonably good view of what the typical recruit experienced. A *second* round of
interviews was more highly structured; the interviews were designed to
focus on the most talked-about areas emerging from the first round. Tape
recordings were made of these second interviews and used as the "voice
over" for the videotaped scenes of recruit life.

Because most attrition from training occurs in the early stages, a
greater proportion of time was devoted to this period. Specific areas included were (1) interaction with the drill instructor, (2) how recruits are
evaluated, e.g., physical fitness tests, academic tests, rifle practice, swim-
ming, and the obstacle course.

College Students

At West Point. Two studies of realistic recruitment have been conducted at the United States Military Academy at West Point. Both studies used booklets to describe experiences of typical cadet life. The first study (Macedonia 1969) used the results from a questionnaire survey of cadets as the basis for realism. This study followed up the entering cadets at the conclusion of their first year at West Point. The second study (Ilgen and Seely 1974) used a modification of the booklet, with the information limited to the summer period prior to the fall term.

Macedonia (1969, pp. 37–39) has described the booklet as follows:

> *It states that the cadet will enter in July and for two months will learn how to be a cadet and a member of the Armed Forces. This period is often referred to as "Beast Barracks." The training is hard and exacting and is designed to develop the qualities of self-discipline and courage—qualities necessary to sustain a leader in combat. And to insure his orderly adjustment to Academy life, it is necessary that he be conscious of the reasons that lie behind his training. None of his training at the academy has been instituted to harass him or to diminish his dignity. Its sole purpose is to fully develop him as a leader. . . .*

> *The second section of the booklet has sketches showing the cadet engaged in each of the various activities available in the fourth class (freshman) year, a brief description of the activity, and the approximate number of hours that each cadet spent in each activity.*

Table 3.1 shows the breakdown, included in the booklet, of how cadets spend their time.

At Barat College. The federal government (Department of Health, Education and Welfare) has given grants to eleven postsecondary schools and four education organizations under a program called "National Task Force on Better Information for Student Choice." The college receiving the most publicity is Barat College, a four-year, liberal arts college for women in Lake Forest, Illinois.

The Barat Prospectus, as it is called, is a 34-page brochure. Some factual material is presented in various tables and charts; e.g., one such chart shows the department-by-department breakdown of faculty size, number

TABLE 3.1

Results of Cadet Time Study—"Typical" Day

Activity	Time (hours)
Class	5
Personal	2-3
Athletics	2-3
Eating	2¼
Sleeping	6-8
Studying	4-5
Extracurricular	1-2
Fourth-class duties	1¾-2½

Also included in section two of the booklet is a copy of the formal schedule of a schoolday:

Activity	Reporting Time
Reveille	0550
Police call	0620
Breakfast	0630
Return to quarters	0715
Class	0745
Dinner	1210
Class	1305
Intramurals (sports)	1535
Supper	1830
Study	1920
Lights-out	2300

Source: R. M. Macedonia, 1969. Expectations: press and survival. Unpublished doctoral dissertation, New York University, p. 39.

of courses offered, number of students, class sizes, and library priority (i.e., the priority the library has placed on new book orders). The bulk of the prospectus, however, is not devoted to charts and tables but gives factual descriptions of various programs of study, student services, background on faculty, the current status of the library, the type of students attending Barat, and the results of a questionnaire study of students—both the best- and least-liked features of life at Barat are listed. A detailed

question-and-answer format is used to handle 19 questions about financial aid, followed by the budgets of three different, but representative,
students.

The overall tenor of the Barat prospectus is positive, but some negative characteristics are included, e.g., "Barat is not notably distinguished
for its use of instructional technology" (Marchese 1976, p. 13). Perhaps
the biggest criticism one can make of the prospectus is that there is so
much information that students may have trouble sifting through it to
determine whether or not Barat is the right place for them. An improvement would have been to analyze the reasons for satisfaction and turnover
among students and highlight only those found to be the *most* important.
Unlike the two studies at West Point, there are no follow-up data from
Barat to assess the effectiveness of the prospectus.

REALISTIC WORK–SAMPLE TESTS:
A VARIATION OF REALISTIC RECRUITMENT

Realistic recruitment practices are designed to operate in parallel with the
selection procedures used by an organization. In fact, all the examples described thus far have reinforced this distinction. However, the dichotomy
between recruitment and selection is not really absolute, as can be seen in
the example of *realistic work-sample tests*.

The popular image of personnel selection procedures seems to be that
paper-and-pencil tests are used to assess basic abilities of job candidates.
The assessment of abilities is then compared with the results of a *job
analysis* assessment of those abilities required for success on a particular
job. Depending on the degree of fit, a person is then either hired or rejected. This image of personnel selection as primarily psychological testing
is also reinforced by current controversies over issues of unfair discrimination in testing. [See Arvey (1979) for examples of this.]

Not all selection procedures follow paper-and-pencil psychological
tests. To develop a realistic work-sample test, the testing situation must be
as similar to actual working conditions as possible. Work-sample tests can
be classified into two categories: verbal and manual (or motor skills). They
are designed for a *specific job,* rather than standardized and used across a
wide variety of situations (such as intelligence tests). Table 3.2 shows a
few examples from the wide variety of verbal and manual work-sample
tests.

TABLE 3.2

Examples of realistic work-sample tests

Verbal

Leaderless group discussion for business supervisors
Leaderless group discussion for military trainees
Manufacturing business game for managers
In-basket test for managers
Speech interview for foreign students
Writing business letters for supervisors
Graph reading and interpolation for students in optometry
Life insurance information for salespeople

Manual

Carving dexterity for dental students
Sewing machine test for operators
Rudder control test for pilots
Code test for radio operators
Typing test for office personnel
The road test for a driver's license
Map reading test for traffic control officers
Optical test for relay adjusters who work with small parts and tools
Programming test for computer programmers

Source: Adapted from J. J. Asher and J. A. Sciarrino, 1974. Realistic work samples: a review. *Personnel Psychology* **27**: 519–533.

A review of these realistic work-sample tests used two types of criteria to evaluate them: (1) how well they predicted success in training for the job, and (2) how well they predicted actual on-the-job performance (Asher and Sciarrino 1974). They found that manual (or motor) work-samples tests were most strongly related to actual job performance, whereas verbal tests were more strongly related to success in training. Besides these comparisons, the authors of the review also compared realistic work-sample tests with more "traditional" selection tests, such as intelligence tests, personality tests, and tests of mechanical aptitude. Manual work-sample tests were better predictors of job performance than these other procedures. Intelligence tests were next best, whereas personality tests were consistently the worst indicator of future job performance. Verbal work-sample tests fell in between intelligence tests and personality tests.

The research on realistic work-sample tests rarely includes an assessment of job satisfaction or voluntary turnover; up to now the focus has been on job performance only. Undoubtedly this stems from the kinds of distinctions made earlier between recruitment and selection (see Fig. 2.1). Two recent studies, however, are exceptions to this trend. Both were realistic work-sample tests for sewing machine operators (Downs, Farr, and Colbeck 1978; O'Leary and Bartlett 1973). The Downs et al. study found that job candidates were excellent judges of their own performance on the realistic work-sample test, even though they were *not* told their own scores. That is, those who scored highest on the test almost always accepted a job offer (91 percent). However, those who scored lowest accepted a job offer at a much lower rate (23 percent). Unfortunately, no job survival nor job performance data were reported. The other study of sewing machine operators (Farr et al. 1973) will be discussed shortly.

In summary, realistic work-sample tests differ from realistic recruitment in certain respects, but may be similar in others. One major difference is that the typical purpose of the work-sample tests has typically been to select rather than recruit newcomers. This has meant that studies that evaluated the usefulness of realistic work-sample tests have *not* looked at effects on job satisfaction, organizational commitment, and voluntary turnover. Instead, they focused on job training success and job performance. The one study that did examine turnover did not report how well the work-sample test operated as a predictor of job performance. Thus no study of realistic work-sample tests has considered the overall impact on all components of the Matching Model.

A second difference is that realistic work-sample tests are given to job candidates *after* the person is already midway in the entry process, after completion of an application form, and after an interview. The longer an organization waits to do any type of realistic recruitment, the greater the risk that it will fall on "deaf ears" because people can become committed to taking the job no matter what they are told. This occurs because the *effort* expended by individuals during entry needs to be *justified*—and what better way to do so than to rationalize that the job is really worth the effort? (Lewis 1965)

One of the most popular selection procedures today is the *assessment center*. [See Moses and Byham (1977) for comprehensive coverage of details.] Since it is primarily used to *select* job candidates, detailed discussion of it is reserved for Chapter 5. It is relevant at this point in the book because the realism built into the simulations used in the assessment center may also have an impact similar to realistic recruitment. To date, however, the critical evaluation of the assessment center has examined its effects on predicting job performance. In this sense it has been treated as a typical realistic work-sample test. Clearly, there is a need to expand our view of how the assessment center and other realistic work-sample tests affect the entry and retention of newcomers.

EVALUATION OF REALISTIC RECRUITMENT

The evaluation of realistic recruitment involves a discussion of what factors should be considered and includes an analysis of the results accumulated to date.

Factors to Be Evaluated

A wide variety of criteria is potentially available for use in an evaluation of realistic recruitment. (See Table 3.3.) At one time or another, all of these have been used, although only rarely has a single study used all six of them at the same time. These six criteria will be used to assess the impact of realistic recruitment.

The six criteria are arranged in a time sequence running from preentry, through entry, to postentry. The first of these is whether or not realism will hamper the ability of an organization to attract competent newcomers. The usual way to assess this is to examine how many applicants there are both before and after the use of realistic recruitment. Simply examining the raw numbers of applicants is not the best way to evaluate this area, however. This is because one must take into account the number of *high-quality* applicants, i.e., those who are matched appropriately to the organization. Because of the difficulties involved in making this quality judgment, usual practice has been to simply analyze the trend in the overall number of applicants.

During the entry stage, the impact of realistic recruitment on *both* initial expectations and on the organizational choice made by the person must be considered. Since the basic purpose of realism is to *deflate* expectations, there should be an assessment made to see whether or not this

TABLE 3.3

Some possible criteria to use in the evaluation of realistic recruitment

STAGE OF ENTRY	TYPE OF CRITERIA
Preentry	1. Ability of the organization to recruit newcomers
Entry	2. Initial expectations of newcomers
	3. Choice of organization by the individual, i.e., needs being matched with climate.
Postentry	4. Initial job attitudes such as:
	• satisfaction with one's job
	• commitment to the organization
	• descriptive statements about the job (to be compared with the expectations held as an outsider)
	• thoughts about quitting
	5. Job performance
	6. Job survival, and voluntary turnover rates

actually happens. One way to do this is to measure the expectations of newcomers both before and after realistic recruitment. Another way is to set up an experiment in which there are two groups, the realistic recruits and the traditional recruits, and compare their expectations. The second area to be evaluated during entry is the extent to which the newcomer actually chooses an organization consistent with the type of information available at the time of choice. This means that job candidates tend to choose organizations whose *advertised image* is similar to the *needs* of the job candidates. When traditional recruitment is used, organizations tend to admit newcomers who are *not* matched well to the various climates of the organization because the wrong types of individuals are attracted. Realistic recruitment attracts those newcomers who will be well matched.

Finally, in the postentry period three other areas need to be evaluated. First, a variety of "job attitudes" should be measured. Both job satisfaction and organizational commitment data are good indicators of the degree to which the individual's needs are matched to the organization's need-reinforcing climates. Follow-up *descriptions* of the organization are gathered to be compared with the *expectations* data gathered earlier. When realistic recruitment is used, there should be little difference between the two. When traditional recruitment is practiced, the initial expectations should be inflated with respect to postentry perceptions of the organization. Finally, thoughts about quitting should be measured. Oftentimes this question will show a difference between realistic and traditional recruitment practices when there is little or no difference in actual turnover between the two. This is most likely to happen during periods of high unemployment that make it difficult for individuals to leave one organization for another.

The last two areas for evaluation during postentry are job performance and job survival. Both of these are key components of the Matching Model. This model, however, does predict that the effect of realistic recruitment is much more evident on voluntary turnover than on job performance because it directly affects the matching of human needs and organizational climates. Nevertheless, both types of data should be obtained to evaluate realistic versus traditional recruitment.

The Impact of Realistic Recruitment

Thirteen experiments have been conducted in various types of organizations on the impact of realistic recruitment. Table 3.4 shows the basic characteristics of each one. For the most part each study included a relatively large number of subjects. The number of subjects shown in Table 3.4 is the total for both realistic and traditional groups of new recruits.

A wide variety of methods was used to present the realistic information during the preview: (1) a work-sample test (once), (2) audiovisual (three times), (3) oral presentations (four times), and (4) booklets (five times). The "timing" of the previews also varied among the thirteen experiments. Only three of the thirteen were clearly *previews* in that the realistic recruitment information was given very early in the organizational entry process. Three others presented the job preview information later on, but prior to final acceptance of an offer by the organization The remaining seven experiments were done on newcomers who had already accepted job offers from the organizations. In Chapter 2 an elaborate model (Fig 2.5) of how realism "works" was shown. Since more than half of these experiments were done *after* candidates accepted job offers, the "self-selection" matching of needs to organizational climate could *not* be a factor in the effect of realism on the subsequent behavior of the newcomers.

TABLE 3.4
Characteristics of realistic job preview experiments

STUDY	SAMPLE			EXPERIMENTAL PROCEDURES		
	SIZE	SEX	JOB TYPE	BASIS FOR REALISM	MEANS USED	TIMING OF PREVIEW
Farr, O'Leary, and Bartlett (1973)	$N = 160$	F	Sewing machine operators at Manhattan Industries, Inc.	Two-hour simulated work experience on sewing machine.	$N = 80$ who were tested and did the simulation. $N = 40$ who were tested only. $N = 40$ who were neither tested nor did the simulation.	Prior to formal job offer acceptance.
Haccoun (1978)	$N = 1,033$ applicants, of which $N = 235$ actually hired and monitored for six months.	M and F (89% F)	Telephone operators at Bell Canada.	Semistructured interviews conducted with $N = 40$ operators. A second sample of operators ($N = 30$) judged the final realistic previews as a check on the accuracy of procedures.	Two types of realistic preview were used (booklet and automatically narrated slide show. A control group saw no previews.	The two preview formats were each used both before and after the selection interview, resulting in four experimental preview groups in all.
Horner (1979)	$N = 678$	M	New recruits to the Marine Corps.	Two series of interviews with recruits from three stages of entry: Prior to training, during training	Eighty-minute videotape of recruit training scenes with "voice over"	After a recruit was in the Marines, but prior to training.

64

Study	N	Sex	Sample/Setting		Procedure	Timing
				and after training. Drill instructors and officers interviewed once.	comments from interviews with recruits. Three groups were studied: (1) realistic preview (N = 174), (2) no preview (N = 330) and (3) no preview of training, but saw a film on the history of this organization. (N = 174)	
Ilgen and Dugoni (1977)	N = 320	M and F	Checkers and baggers in a retail chain in the midwest	Employees (N = 130) answered an open-ended questionnaire asking them to describe best and least satisfying experiences.	Employees randomly split into a 30-minute realistic preview as part of a two-hour orientation (N = 169) vs. those who got only the 1.5-hour company orientation (N = 151). Preview information presented orally by one of the researchers to groups of 30 at a time.	After accepting a job offer, but one month prior to the first day at work.

(continued)

TABLE 3.4 (Cont.)

| STUDY | SAMPLE | | | EXPERIMENTAL PROCEDURES | | |
	SIZE	SEX	JOB TYPE	BASIS FOR REALISM	MEANS USED	TIMING OF PREVIEW
Ilgen and Seely (1974)	$N = 468$	M	Cadets at the United States Military Academy at West Point.	Revision of the Macedonia (1969) booklet based on interviews with cadets and officers.	Booklet distributed by mail to $N = 234$ cadets. Another $N = 234$ were selected at random as the control.	After written acceptance of appointments, but prior to entry and oath at the two-month summer training program.
Krausz and Fox (1979)	$N = 54$	M and F	Psychology undergraduates at an Israeli University.	Surveys of student opinions and the teaching experience of the two authors were used.	Twenty-minute oral presentation by a psychology faculty member given in three different types of previews: (1) negative ($N = 19$), (2) positive ($N = 14$), and (3) balanced ($N = 12$) A no-preview group ($N = 11$) was also used.	After admittance to and acceptance of the program, but prior to the first day of classes.
Macedonia (1969)	$N = 1,260$	M	Cadets at the United States Military Academy at	Questionnaire survey of freshmen on time usage and of seniors on per-	Booklet distributed by mail to $N = 568$ cadets and not to	After written acceptance of appointment, but prior to entry and oath at

Parkington and Schneider (1978)	$N = 36$	M and F	West Point.	ceived climate.	the remaining $N = 692$.	the two-month summer training program.
			Introductory psychology students performing on a one-hour laboratory task to evaluate credit card applications.	Previews of task written by researchers and checked by 15 outside judges independently for accuracy of each preview. A very high degree of agreement among judges was reached when they sorted the previews into one of the three categories.	Previews given to subjects during a telephone conversation. Three preview groups: (1) realistic general information, (2) realistic task-specific information, and (3) traditional general and nonnegative information. A second vaccination of previews was given upon arrival at the experiment It was an abbreviated version of the one given over the phone.	After a subject volunteered and after the subject was accepted into the experimental task. The time between the preview and the task was one to two days.

[handwritten marginalia:] time too short for guy cue — labstudy

(continued)

TABLE 3.4 (Cont.)

| STUDY | SAMPLE | | | EXPERIMENTAL PROCEDURES | | |
	SIZE	SEX	JOB TYPE	BASIS FOR REALISM	MEANS USED	TIMING OF PREVIEW
Wanous (1973) n.s.	$N = 80$	F	Telephone operators at Southern New England Telephone.	Questionnaire survey of experienced operators, interviews with operators and supervisors, and personal observation.	Two films used: the company's recruiting film and a new realistic film both 15 minutes long.	After job offer, but prior to formal acceptance of it.
Weitz (1956) offer	$N = 474$	M	Life insurance agents at Life and Casualty Insurance Company of Tennessee.	Questionnaire survey of experienced agents.	Booklet mailed to prospective agents.	Prior to the organization's selection decisions.
Youngberg (1963) offer	$N = 404$	M	Life insurance agents at the Prudential Insurance Company.	Not specified, but said to be similar to the one used earlier by Weitz.	Booklet mailed to applicants.	Prior to organization's selection decision. Some people had early orientation training as well as the booklet.

	N	Sex	Sample	Method	Treatment	Timing
Gomersall and Myers (1966)	$N = 20$ in pretest; $N = 200$ in final experiment	F	Operatives at Texas Instruments.	Interviews with workers and two levels of supervision. Questionnaire completed by employees of varying lengths of tenure.	An "anxiety reduction" session held on the first day following the standard two-hour company orientation by the personnel department Given orally to the newcomers.	After acceptance of a job offer, during the first day on the job.
Reilly, Tenopyr, and Sperling (1979)	$N = 325$	Predominately female	Telephone operator	Interviews with operators yielded a long list of statements. These were then rated by $N = 305$ operators for: (1) accuracy, and (2) favorableness.	Two booklets: (1) a realistic booklet containing 36 favorable and 21 unfavorable statements, (2) a traditional booklet containing 36 favorable and 21 neutral statements A "control group" did not receive either booklet.	After the selection test, but prior to a job offer.

The results of these thirteen experiments[1] are shown in Table 3.5. Five studies examined the impact of realism on the organization's ability to recruit newcomers. All five found that realism had no negative impact here. Since many personnel managers worry about this, these results are significant in dispelling a widely held belief that realism may drive away job candidates.

The first effect of realism (see Fig. 2.5) is supposed to be in the *vaccination* of expectations, which usually means the *lowering* of *inflated* expectations. Of the thirteen studies, five actually measured the impact of realistic recruitment on these initial expectations. All five found that the previews lowered expectations. In fact, one of them (Wanous 1973) found that only those expectations of concern in the preview were lowered. Other beliefs, not addressed in the preview, were unaffected. This is important because it is one indication that realistic recruitment presents *selective* information and is *not* a "general turnoff" for job candidates. The absence of a spillover of realism should be encouraging to companies contemplating the installation of realistic recruitment. Finally, there is little evidence that realism has any negative impact on acceptance of a job offer, since four of five students found that realism did not adversely affect job offer acceptance rates.

Three types of postentry evaluations can be made of these realistic recruitment experiments. First, what impact was there on various types of job attitudes? Six studies measured these. Three found attitudes to be more positive for the realistic recruits, and three found no differences. Second, what was the impact on job performance? Realism appears to have little or not effect here. Eight of the eleven looked at various measures of job performance. Of these eight, four found no differences between realistic recruits and other newcomers; one found lower performance for realistic recruits; three found higher performance for realistic recruits. On balance, the Matching Model is supported by these results because job performance should really not be affected as much by recruitment as it should by selection.

The final area for evaluating realistic recruitment is in the effect it

---

[1] The *p*-values in parentheses in Table 3.5 refer to the level of statistical significance. Generally, a result of $p = .05$ or lower is considered "significant" because the odds are only 1 in 20 that the difference found between the two groups is an error. The entry (n.s.) means "not significant."

has on the job survival of newcomers. Since one of the experiments was a laboratory study of one-hour duration, job survival was not a relevant consideration. Of the remaining twelve studies, nine found that job survival was longer for realistic recruits than for others. Three others found little or no difference. However, in one of these the authors themselves question the accuracy of the organization's records (Krausz and Fox 1979) and in the other there were so many being fired that there were very few *voluntary* quits (Ilgen and Dugoni 1977). It must be remembered that realistic recruitment is aimed at reducing voluntary, not involuntary, turnover. Thus it is safe to conclude that realism does have demonstrated beneficial effects without high costs to the organization.

Other Studies of Realism

At the end of Chapter 2 Fig. 2.5 presents a diagram of how realism seems to reduce turnover. One of the mechanisms was the "vaccination effect" that realism can have on the expectations of job candidates. The idea is that individuals will have less regret about making a decision if they can anticipate the probable negative consequences of making it than they will have if they are naive in their expectations.

Deciding to join an organization is one type of decision, but there are many others. Another category of decisions concerns those that require a person to experience short-term discomfort in order to satisfy a long-term goal. Personal health problems are a good example of this type of decision because they are fertile ground for feeling regret about one's choice to undergo painful surgery, for example. Thus the emotional preparations of patients in hospitals for discomfort can be another application of vaccination through realism.

A recent study of the psychological processes found in decision making (Janis and Mann 1977) mentions ten field experiments using realistic preparation in the personal health area. Seven of the ten were of patients about to undergo surgery (Egbert, Battit, Welch, and Bartlett 1964; Johnson 1966; Moran 1963; Schmidt 1966; Schmitt and Woolridge 1973; Vernon and Bigelow 1974; and Wolfer and Visintainer 1975). The other three were of women about to undergo childbirth (Levy and McGee 1975), patients about to have a tooth extracted (Miller and Treiger 1976), and hospitalized patients about to have an unpleasant medical examination (Johnson and Leventhal 1974).

TABLE 3.5

Results of realistic job preview experiments

| STUDY | PREENTRY | ENTRY | | POSTENTRY | | |
	ABILITY TO RECRUIT	INITIAL EXPECTATIONS	CHOICE OF ORGANIZATION BY PERSON	ATTITUDES	PERFORMANCE	JOB SURVIVAL
Farr, O'Leary, and Bartlett (1973)	Not measured	Not measured	Slightly higher refusal rates for realistic group (n.s.)	Not measured	Not measured	88.9% vs. 60% ($p < .05$) for six wks, and 88.9% vs. 68.8% ($p < .11$) for four wks.
Haccoun (1978)	No differences across the five groups in job refusal rates after seeing the preview, nor were any subsequent differences found when operators could have interviewed for other jobs.	Not measured	Not measured	Not measured	Seeing any type of preview resulted in being rated as having a "favorable attitude" during training and after four months on the job. These results were most pronounced for those in the audiovisual group who saw the preview before the interview. No differ-	No differences among groups.

					...ences on any other performance measure were found.
Horner (1979)	Not measured	The expectations of the realistic preview group were more likely to be confirmed by actual experiences, as compared with the expectations of the other groups.	Not measured	Those in the realistic preview group had greater role clarity, but there were no differences in satisfaction, commitment, or thoughts of quitting in comparison with the other groups.	The realistic preview group performed better ($p < .001$) in acquiring military skills during three months of training.	89.7% vs. 85.1% ($p < .17$) for three months. After both six months and one year, however, the number of job survival days was greater for these in the realistic preview group ($p < .05$) than the other groups.
Ilgen and Dugoni (1977)	Not measured	The negative information lowered expectations, but the positive component of the preview was about equal to the initial expectations of the no preview group.	Not measured	No consistent differences between the two groups after two to three months of work experience.	Of the original 320 persons, 128 (40%) were fired during the first two months. No differences between the two groups were found, however.	Voluntary turnover was only 9% for the first two months. No differences between the two groups were found, however.

(continued)

TABLE 3.5 (Cont.)

STUDY	PREENTRY	ENTRY			POSTENTRY		
	ABILITY TO RECRUIT	INITIAL EXPECTATIONS	CHOICE OF ORGANIZATION BY PERSON	ATTITUDES	PERFORMANCE	JOB SURVIVAL	
Ilgen and Seely (1974)	Not measured	Not measured	4.5% of realistic group withdrew prior to two month summer training program but no rate for the no preview group was reported.	Not measured	Not measured	94% vs. 88.5% ($p < .05$) for two months.	
Krausz and Fox (1979)	Not measured	Slight tendency for expectations to be in the rank order predicted by the three levels of preview informa- tion. No dif- ference be- tween the no preview group and the balanced preview group.	Not measured	No differences at 4.5 months later in either satisfaction or expectations. Sample sizes had shrunk from $N = 45$ in the three preview groups to $N = 28$ at 4.5 months postentry.	Not measured	No differences among the vari- ous groups, but authors question the quality of these data.	

Study						
Macedonia (1969)	Not measured	Not measured	10.6% of realistic group declined vs. 21.1% for no preview (p < .01).	Not measured	Peer ratings of realistic recruits lower than for others (p < .10).	91.3% vs. 86.1% (p < .01) for one year.
Parkington and Schneider (1978)	No one declined to participate during the one to two day interval between the preview and the task.	Not measured	Not measured	The more realistic the information, the greater the satisfaction (r = .32, p < .05). Realism was not related to feelings of regret at having participated.	Realism not related to performance.	No one left before the end of the experiment.
Wanous (1973)	No difference between groups	Lower for realistic group than no preview (p < .05). No difference for those facets omitted from the films.	No difference between groups.	Thoughts of quitting lower for realistic than no preview group (p < .05) after one month.	No difference between groups	62% vs. 50% (n.s.) for three months.

(continued)

TABLE 3.5 (Cont.)

| STUDY | PREENTRY | ENTRY | | | POSTENTRY | |
	ABILITY TO RECRUIT	INITIAL EXPECTATIONS	CHOICE OF ORGANIZATION BY PERSON	ATTITUDES	PERFORMANCE	JOB SURVIVAL
Weitz (1956)	No difference between groups	Not measured	Not measured	Not measured	Not measured	81% vs. 73% ($p < .05$) for all time periods together. 68% vs. 53% for six months (n.s.).
Youngberg (1963)	9% more agents hired in realistic group (n.s.).	Slightly more realistic for realistic group than no preview group (n.s.).	Not measured	80% vs. 64% "satisfied" at the end of three months ($p < .001$).	No difference between groups	89% vs. 84% ($p < .10$) for three months. 71% vs. 57% ($p < .01$) for six months.
Gomersall and Myers (1966)	Not measured	Not measured	Not measured	Not measured	Exact data not reported, but authors claim that productivity, quality of work, and learning time all favorably improved by realism. Performance increased about 50% in realistic group.	Absenteeism rate was .5% for realistic group vs. 2.5% for traditional group during first month on the job. Tardiness less for realistic group. No job survival data available, but authors say turnover was reduced.

Reilly, Tenopyr, and Sperling (1979)	Not measured	Not measured	Job acceptance rates were: 56.1% for the realistic group, 68.6% for the favorable group and 71.6% for the control group ($p < .05$)	Not measured	Not measured	87.5% vs. 77.1% for one month ($p < .05$), but 89.7% for the control group. After six months it was 56.2% vs. 61.4% and 64.1% for the control group (n.s.) When only voluntary turnover was considered, 9.4% of the realistic group quit vs. 10.0% for the favorable group and 15.4% for the control group (n.s.).

Although the "vaccinated" groups of patients were better adjusted during the recovery period, they tended to be more agitated than those (naive) patients not exposed to realistic expectations. In essence, they worried about the impending operation and began to develop *coping strategies,* e.g., convincing themselves that the operation was worth it in the long run and that the discomfort would be only temporary.

Although these studies of realism in hospitals are similar to studies of realistic recruitment, there are several important differences. First the hospital studies focused on how realism affected such factors as the degree of pain reported by patients, the amount of pain-relieving drugs administered, and the length of the patient's stay in the hospital. It is rather difficult to compare these factors with those associated with entry into and withdrawal from organizations. There is no separation of factors leading to voluntary versus involuntary turnover, as shown in the dual matching processes in the Matching Model.

A second difference between the hospital studies and those described in Tables 3.4 and 3.5 is that most hospital studies were done on very small samples of people. All of the hospital studies examined fewer than 100 patients; the smallest examined only 15.

The final difference between the hospital studies and those of new employees concerns the reasons why realism has beneficial effects. Some studies of realistic recruitment tried to test out the theory expressed in Fig. 2.5. In contrast to this, none of the hospital studies attempted to evaluate why realism has beneficial effects.

Other Applications of Realism

Based on the research conducted thus far, providing realistic preparatory information to job candidates and hospital patients does seem to be useful. Realistic information may also be effective when supplied in other situations, although little or no research has yet been attempted. Nevertheless, it seems a logical extension to expect realistic preparatory information to facilitate other types of employment transitions: (1) the transfer of personnel to new geographical areas, particularly to overseas assignments, and (2) the transfer of employees to new, challenging job assignments. Some transfers, of course, may involve both types of changes—geographical and job duties.

An area of increasing concern to large, multinational corporations is the successful transfer of highly paid technicians and executives to foreign countries. The transfer costs are extremely high. They can run to six figures for an executive who requests a return home after a short, unhappy experience in a foreign country.

In today's business climate, companies are increasingly willing to accept an employee's refusal of a geographical transfer. Given this, it is even more crucial that realistic information be provided to personnel as inputs to the decision about accepting or rejecting a transfer. The realistic information can operate in two ways. First, realism may convince an executive to refuse a transfer, and thereby save the company money because an error was prevented. Second, realism may induce a reluctant employee to accept a transfer by showing the employee that his or her fears about the move are unrealistic. Given the greater number of transfer refusals today, this latter effect may be quite significant in reducing employee resistance to changes in life-style caused by geographical transfers.

In a likewise manner realistic preparatory information can be used to facilitate the matching of person and job when it is used to decide transfers to a more difficult job assignment within an organization. The only difference between this and realistic recruitment is that the movement is entirely internal, rather than being a shift from outside to inside an organization. Because of this difference in focus, the realistic information provided in an internal transfer concerns new job duties, new co-workers, and new working conditions. Of less concern in preparing someone for internal transfer are those factors that pervade the entire organization; they, of course, are included in the realistic job preview during recruitment.

PRACTICAL GUIDELINES FOR REALISTIC RECRUITMENT

In this section attention is focused on two practical considerations in the use of realistic recruitment. The first of these concerns the basic decision about whether or not to use this recruitment strategy. It includes discussion of: (1) the organization's selection ratio, (2) the types of jobs to be filled, and (3) the effects of labor market unemployment on realistic recruitment. The second area to be considered concerns factors that should be taken into account *after* a decision has been made to go ahead with realistic recruitment. It includes (1) the type of medium used to present realistic information, (2) a caution about arousing needs for achievement in job candidates, (3) the timing of the realistic job preview during entry, (4) the optimal level of realism to use, and (5) a reminder that realistic recruitment is *not* a substitute for desirable change in organizations.

When Should Realism Be Used?

Earlier in this chapter considerable attention was paid to both the types of symptoms that should be monitored and the various methods for doing so. In this section the focus is on limitations in the use of realism since it is *not* an appropriate recruitment strategy for all types of jobs.

Selection ratio. Realistic recruitment can be best used in those situations where the selection ratio is low, i.e., a small percentage of those seeking a job are actually hired. This, however, is a basic limitation on virtually all types of recruitment/selection/placement practices used by organizations. It makes relatively little sense to spend the personnel budget in areas of high cost per person. The procedure to evaluate the cost effectiveness of changes in entry procedures is beyond the scope of this book, but has been discussed elsewhere by Janz and Dunnette (1977).

Type of job. Positions at the entry level into the organization are the best targets for realism. This is because those coming from outside to inside an organization have more greatly inflated expectations than those who make job changes internally. When outsiders enter new organizations, they must learn about both the specific job and the broader organizational climate. When insiders move, they have better information based on their own experiences, they have more sources of information (i.e., they don't have to rely on recruiters), and they are not subjected to the same types of conflicts (Fig. 2.2) between individual and organization over the "dual processes of attraction and choice."

The unemployment rate. Having a realistic preview that is "too late" is one way to reduce its effectiveness. Having high unemployment is another because it limits the number of viable options open to job candidates. When this occurs the impact of realism is almost certainly limited to an expectations vaccination.

Guidelines for Installation of Realistic Recruitment

Assuming that the decision has been made to implement a realistic strategy, at least four factors must be considered during the installation.

Medium used. In the review of those studies that have tried realism, it was clear that many different methods were used: audiovisual techniques, booklets, work samples, and oral presentations. In fact the point was emphasized that realistic recruitment is a philosophy rather than a specific technique. Some people might have incorrectly concluded from this that the means used are thus irrelevant. Yet nothing could be further from the truth! The results shown in Table 3.5 clearly indicate that an oral presentation is the least effective means for doing realistic recruitment. In other cases the medium used can simply overpower the intended message, as described below in another example from SNET.

The procedures used to help operator candidates decide about a job offer included a job visit (see Fig. 3.2) as part of the normal entry procedures. The intended purpose of this was to show a candidate the actual working conditions during a 30–60-minute tour. Question asking was, of course, encouraged. The company reasoned that nothing could be more realistic than an on-site tour. The appeal of this reasoning was strong, but it overlooked the fact that a *short* visit was not the best way to communicate the *long-term* effects of being on this job. A short visit created the impression of high job challenge (not confirmed by subsequent work experience) and of high work variety (also not confirmed).

Arousal of other motives. Some uses of realism (see the description for life insurance agents quoted earlier) go so far as to pose tough, but surmountable, challenges to job candidates. When this is done, the organization runs the risk of attracting newcomers with strong needs for achievement. This may be perfectly fine *if* the job is characterized by achievement-oriented conditions.[2] Otherwise it will attract only newcomers who will be poorly matched. The important thing is to try to reflect the job and organizational conditions as accurately as possible, using a wide variety of information as the basis for the preview.

---

[2] The three conditions conducive to satisfaction of high achievement needs are (1) moderate challenge or risk, (2) concrete feedback on one's performance, and (3) high personal responsibility for actions (McClelland et al. 1957).

Timing of the preview, The location of realism in the entry process has a very clear impact on how potent a force it can be on subsequent turnover. The general rule-of-thumb is to place the realistic information *as early in the entry process as possible.*

Take the telephone operator study at SNET as a case example. The location of the realistic preview (see Fig. 3.2) was about midway during entry. This decision was made for cost considerations; i.e., to do it earlier would have meant showing the films to at least twice as many people. The result of this timing of the realistic preview was to *lessen* its impact on the individual's choice of (and subsequent commitment to) the organization. This happened because the job candidates had already invested much personal effort, and had even gotten a job offer, by the time the job preview film was shown to them. Psychologists have shown that effort expenditure enhances the attractiveness of a particular action (Lewis 1965). Thus the operator recruits at SNET tended to enhance the attractiveness of the job to justify their own efforts in seeking it out. In fact, only two out of 80 operators actually rejected the job offer. This is a clear indication that SNET's realistic preview was timed "too late" to influence the individual's own choice of the organization. Thus the most likely explanation of why turnover was reduced at SNET is the *vaccination* of *expectations*. (See Fig. 2.5.)

There is an optimal level of realism. The danger of providing too little realism to recruits has been a major theme of this chapter. It would be wrong, however, for an organization to assume that "more is better" where realism is concerned. The primary danger here is creating such a negative situation that recruitment is actually hampered. The primary psychological danger is to make the recruit feel helpless to avoid the negative situation (Janis and Mann 1977). The best advice given by Janis and Mann (1977, p. 390) is that

> . . . *preparatory communications can be expected to be effective only if they arouse vigilance and, at the same time, help build up the person's confidence that he can cope. . . .*

Realistic recruitment is not a substitute for organizational change. The role of recruitment has been the focus of Chapters 2 and 3 and it may appear (incorrectly) that recruitment is a potent means to increase organizational effectiveness and personal satisfaction. Realistic recruitment is *not* a substitute for good selection procedures; it is complementary to selection. It also is clearly *not* a substitute for needed organizational changes. Job conditions that cause undesirable turnover must also be changed. [See Hackman (1977) for a discussion of how work may be redesigned.] Simply alerting newcomers to the negative conditions is not a long-run solution. If one examines the differences in job survival rates for the realistic versus traditional groups (Table 3.5), one can see a gap between them. However, it is also important to examine the overall levels of job survival. Even though realism consistently reduces turnover, the gains are modest, suggesting that organizations probably need to change working conditions to achieve further reduction in unnecessary turnover.

CONCLUSIONS

1. Ineffective recruitment can affect either the job *performance* of newcomers (and thus involuntary turnover) or it can affect the *job satisfaction* or *organizational commitment* of newcomers (and thus voluntary turnover). The primary impact of *recruitment,* however, is on the latter, not the former. Organizational *selection* practices affect the former. (See Conclusion 6.)

2. The diagnosis of the need to use realistic recruitment should include a variety of methods to obtain data. For example, both interviews and questionnaire surveys have been used. A wide variety of data sources should be used, e.g., supervisors, both experienced and inexperienced jobholders, and personal observation.

3. Realistic recruitment is *not* a specific technique. It is a general philosophy or approach to dealing with newcomers. Several methods of presenting realistic job preview information have included audiovisual techniques (films, videotape, and automatically narrated slide presentations), booklets, oral presentations, and realistic work-sample tests.

4. Realistic recruitment does *not* reduce an organization's ability to recruit newcomers.

5. Realistic recruitment deflates the recruits' expectations, which are typically inflated. The most common consequence of this is more positive job attitudes for newcomers.

6. Realistic recruitment has no effect on the job performance of new-comers. This is consistent with the Matching Model. (See Conclusion 1.)

7. Realistic recruitment *does,* however, increase the job survival rate for newcomers.

8. In deciding whether or not to use realistic recruitment, an organization must consider the specific situation: (1) the selection ratio for the job, (2) the type of job, and (3) the unemployment rate. The maximum benefits from realisitc recruitment will occur when it is used for entry-level jobs with a low selection ratio during times of low unemployment.

9. After the decision to use realistic recruitment has been made, several other factors must be considered: (1) the medium used should not contradict the message, (2) needs for achievement might be aroused by realism, (3) the preview should be given early in the entry process, (4) too much realism may cause despair, and (5) realistic recruitment is not a substitute for needed organizational changes.

Choice of an Organization

4

Organizational choice is a stage in the entry process that primarily concerns the individual's perspective. Referring to the Matching Model (Fig. 1.1), organizational choice is the primary way in which human *needs* are matched to the *climates* of an organization. Chapter 5 on selection of newcomers by the organization will focus on how a person's *abilities* are matched to the *requirements* of a job; it is a view of entry from the organization's perspective.

This chapter is divided into six sections. The first section concerns the differences between *organizational* choice and *occupational* entry. Following this, two "case studies" of organizational choice are described. Each of these represents a rather different view of how individuals decide to accept a job offer. The third section reviews research studies in order to evaluate the appropriateness of each view of how organizational choices are made. Fourth, the connection between recruitment and organizational choice is explained. The fifth section assesses impact of job interviews on the job candidates' choice of an organization. The section reviews research from studies of interviewers and interviewees, and suggests several "guidelines" for job candidates. The final section extends the topic of organizational choice to include the individual's decision to leave, i.e., "organizational exit" or voluntary turnover.

ORGANIZATIONAL CHOICE VERSUS VOCATIONAL ENTRY

Much more research and writing is available on the topic of vocational choice, or occupational entry, than is available on organizational choice. The subject of occupational entry is quite broad. For example, it includes the study of how vocational choices are made, how individuals adjust to vocations, the meaning of occupational success, and satisfaction with one's vocation (Crites 1969). Theories abound about how vocational choices are made. Some theories are exclusively psychological; i.e., they try to explain the hows and whys of decisions made by individuals that culminate in vocational entry. Other theories, however, are not so "neatly organized," emphasizing instead the haphazard and accidental way that some people enter particular vocations. Still other theories are sociological, stressing that the *groups* (determined by socioeconomic class, race, or sex) to which one belongs determine occupational entry. Thus one important way that vocational entry differs from organizational choice is that there seems to be *less* agreement among scholars about how people and vocations are matched to each other.

The relationship between organizational choice and vocational entry can be diagrammed as shown in Fig. 4.1. This relationship has been called the "exclusion process" (Crites 1969). It has been so named because the final outcome—a specific job in a particular organization—is the end result of *many choices* made during one's growth into adulthood. An example of a general occupational field would be science. An example of a specific occupation would be research chemist. An example of the job choice would be doing research chemistry on the development of a new additive for gasoline. An example of organizational choice would be choosing to work for Exxon instead of Shell Oil Company.

The "flow" of events pictured in Fig. 4.1 implies three things about the differences between organizational choice and vocational entry. First, one's choice of an organization typically *follows* the entry into a vocation. Second, entry into a vocation is a long, drawnout *process* composed of many "small" decisions and a few "turning points." In contrast, organizational choice is more a single *event* than a long process. Third, it is probably much easier to change organizations than it is to change one's specific occupation, and the hardest to change would be the basic occupational field. Thus most people will probably work for several organizations over

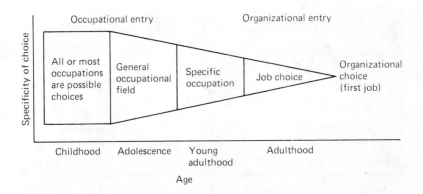

Fig. 4.1 *The narrowing down from occupational entry to organizational entry. (Adapted from J. O. Crites, 1969,* Vocational Psychology, *p. 162. Reprinted by permission of the McGraw-Hill Book Company.)*

their working career, fewer will change jobs, fewer will change to a new occupation, and fewer still will make a radical change to a whole new vocational field.

Actual statistics on the relative frequency of these changes are hard to obtain because changes in a position with an organization may or may not involve a change in one's job, and may or may not involve a change in occupation. The complexity of such changes has plagued research efforts in the area of labor mobility (Parnes 1954; 1970). Based on the 1970 census, we know that 47 percent of the men and 40 percent of the women in the United States were in the same occupation in 1970 as they were in 1965 (*Wall Street Journal,* February 3, 1977). On an overall basis, this seems to be a rather high rate of occupational switching, but there are wide differences among occupations. For example, only 10 percent of the lawyers, doctors, or pharmacists changed in that five-year period compared with 58 percent of garage and gas station workers.

One way to represent the entire process of vocational entry was composed by behavioral scientists from several basic disciplines such as psychology, sociology, and economics, as shown in Fig. 4.2. The key feature of it is the *dual* perspective of both individuals and organizations.

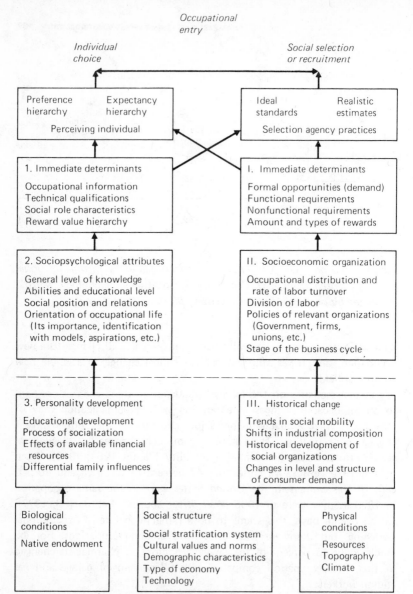

Fig. 4.2 *General framework for occupational entry. (From P. M. Blau, J. W. Gustad, R. Jesson, H. S. Parnes, and R. C. Wilcox, 1956, Occupational choices: a conceptual framework, Industrial and Labor Relations Review 9: 534. Copyright © 1956 by Cornell University.)*

The essence of this model is best described in the authors' own words (Blau et al. 1956, p. 336):

> *Occupational choice, then, can be conceptualized as a process involving a series of decisions to present oneself to employers or other selectors as a candidate for a number of more or less related occupations. Each decision is governed by the way in which the individual compromises his ideal preference and his actual expectations of being able to enter a given occupation, the latter being conditioned by previous rejections and other experiences. Occupational selection, on the other hand, consists of successive decisions of employers (or other selectors) about applicants for jobs. The decision concerning each candidate is guided by the employer's ideal standards and by his estimate of the chances that a better qualified candidate than the one under consideration will present himself in the near future. The process of occupational selection involves a regression from ideal standards (or an increase of rewards), the limits of which are defined by the occupational choices of potential workers. Correspondingly, the process of occupational choice involves a descent in a hierarchy of preferences (or the acquisition of new qualifications), which comes to an end, at least temporarily, by being selected for an occupation.*

The framework has two important characteristics. First, the dual nature of entry means that the entry process is quite often a *compromise* for *both* individuals *and* for organizations. Individuals enter occupations (and organizations) that may *not* be at the top of their list of preferences, because they realize there may be little or no chance for entry into the preferred ones. Similarly, organizations may be able to articulate the description of an ideal job candidate. However, they are faced with real, but imperfect, applicants about whom a decision must be made.

The second important aspect of this framework is that it shows a large number of factors in a developmental sequence. The arrows show the direction of influence one set of factors has on another. The dotted line separates immediate determinants from long-term factors that influence the more concrete and immediate causes of entry.

TWO VIEWS OF ORGANIZATIONAL CHOICE

Those who have studied how people decide which organizations to enter are not in agreement about how these decisions are made. There are essentially two quite different views on the matter. The first view assumes that individuals are reasonably rational beings, that they seek out information about alternative organizations, and that they try to maximize their potential satisfaction by choosing organizations most likely to meet their important needs. The second view of organizational choice assumes that individuals *do not* seek out as much information about organizations. Rather they confine themselves to getting data about only the very most important things they are looking for in a new organization. They use less information and fewer criteria to make organizational choices. Only *after* making a choice do they rationalize the choice in terms of a wider variety of factors.

Two hypothetical "case studies" are presented to highlight these differences in how experts think people choose organizations. The first of these examines the choice process as a systematically rational decision. The case concerns how a graduating senior chooses a graduate business school. In this particular case the person (Bob) is also participating in a research study of how organizational choices are made in which students were asked to complete a questionnaire detailing how they thought about the decision.

Organizational Choice as a Systematic, Rational Decision

The case of Ed was used to open this book. Recall that Ed had graduated from a midwestern university and gone east for his MBA. Let's consider the case of Ed's college roommate, Bob, who was also going on for the MBA degree.

Bob was a good student, but had a lower grade point average than Ed. He also did not score as high on the Graduate Management Admissions Test (GMAT). Whereas Ed had seriously considered only a few high prestige colleges, Bob was forced to face the fact that some of the colleges he chose might reject him.

During the latter part of his senior year, Bob was asked to participate in a study of how students selected a graduate business school. To do this he completed a detailed questionnaire about how he considered the alternatives and made his decision. In the months following this initial questionnaire, Bob received a follow-up questionnaire to assess the degree of correspondence between what he said he would do and what he actually did.

Besides asking for personal background data, the questionnaire included items in three areas: (1) *beliefs* about *expected outcomes* for each school considered, (2) the degree of *importance* of each outcome to Bob, and (3) Bob's *expectancy of being admitted* to a school *if* he made an effort to apply.

The responses Bob gave to the questions are summarized in Table 4.1. Bob was asked to name the several schools he had been thinking about. The four schools Bob listed are shown in Table 4.1. Bob included a Big Ten school, since it was his own school. The Ivy League college was prestigious and was among those his roommate, Ed, had applied to. The local state college was included as a "fall back" option, should he be rejected at all others. Finally, the west coast university was considered because it was a good school located in a desirable area.

Table 4.1 shows Bob's answers to the questions asked about each of the schools. The local state college was the only school he rated low in terms of how much he would probably learn. The cost of the MBA degree varied widely among all four schools, however. Staying close to home would be less expensive than paying the high tuition (and travel costs) of either the Ivy League school or the out-of-state tuition (and travel costs) at the west coast university. Interestingly, Bob was unable to see many differences in the flexibility of each school's program. Thus he rated them all equally at a moderately high level. Finally, he rated the two local schools lower in terms of desirable location than he did either of the out-of-state alternatives.

Having stated his *beliefs* (or perceptions) about *each school,* Bob rated the *importance of each outcome to him.* In this case each outcome received a different rating, but all could have received the same one if that's the way Bob felt. Bob took a long-range view, and rated job prospects as much more important than how much the degree would cost. Not everyone, of course, felt the same way as Bob did.

Finally, Bob was asked to rate his *expectancy of being admitted* to each school if he applied to it. He saw his chances as pretty slim at the Ivy Leaugue school (about 20 percent, or one in five), but excellent at local state college (no chance for rejection).

TABLE 4.1

Organizational choice example: basic data
Beliefs about expected outcomes at each college

Measurement   1.0 = A 100 percent chance of this being true at the college
       .9 = A 90 percent chance of this being true at the college
       .8 = An 80 percent chance of this being true at the college
       ⋮
       0 = Impossible for this to be true.

Results

	COLLEGES CONSIDERED			
QUESTIONS ASKED	BIG TEN	IVY LEAGUE	LOCAL STATE	WEST COAST UNIVERSITY
1. Learn a lot	.8	.9	.4	.8
2. Low cost	.6	0	1.0	.2
3. Good job prospects	.7	1.0	.3	.7
4. Flexible program	.7	.7	.7	.7
5. Desirable geography	.4	.7	.4	.9

Importance of each outcome

Measurement

5 = Extremely important
4 = Very important
3 = Important
2 = Somewhat important
1 = Slightly important
0 = Irrelevant

Results

4   1. Learn a lot
2   2. Low cost
5   3. Good job prospects
1   4. Flexible program
3   5. Desirable geography

Expectancy of being admitted

Measurement

1.0 = A 100% chance of acceptance
  .9 = A 90 % chance of acceptance
  ⋮
  0 = No chance whatsoever

Results

.8   Big Ten school in home state
.2   Ivy League college
1.0   Local state college
.6   West coast university

Taking the raw data provided in Table 4.1, the researchers conducting the organizational choice study combined the data as shown in Table 4.2.

The way in which these data were combined illustrates a theory of how an organizational choice is made. The theory identifies several components: the *attractiveness* of an organization, the *effort* made to enter one, and the *final choice* of an organization from among those that offer admittance. This theory is called *expectancy theory*. (See Nadler and Lawler, 1977, for an easily readable explanation.)

What makes an organization *attractive* to an individual? Two pieces of information are combined in a unique way to indicate the relative attractiveness of the four organizations considered by Bob in the case study: (1) his *beliefs* about *outcomes* associated with each one, and (2) the *importance* of each outcome. As shown in Table 4.2, the attractiveness of an organization can be represented as an algebraic formula:

$$\text{Attractiveness of an organization} = \sum \text{Belief about each outcome} \times \text{Importance of each outcome.}$$

The *attractiveness* of an organization, often called the *preferred* organization, is an important piece of information, but it is *not sufficient* to indicate which schools Bob will actually apply to. To understand where Bob will apply, information about his *expectancy of being admitted* is necessary. At the bottom of Table 4.2, the total attractiveness score for each school is multiplied by the expectancy of admittance to yield Bob's *total motivation to apply to each school*.

$$\text{Total motivation to join an organization} = \text{Expectancy of being admitted to the organization} \times \text{Attractiveness of the organization.}$$

A comparison of the rank orders of attractiveness and of total motivation shows important differences. The Ivy League college was the most attractive to Bob, but he may not even apply to it! According to expectancy theory, Bob will certainly apply to the Big Ten university, since it is tops in *total* motivation. The local state college and the west coast university, although lower in total motivation, will also probably receive applications from Bob. Whether he will apply to the Ivy League college is *not clear*.

TABLE 4.2
Organizational choice example: how the model operates

Calculating the attractiveness of each college

TYPE OF OUTCOME	BIG TEN UNIVERSITY BELIEF × IMPORTANCE = ATTRACTIVENESS	IVY LEAGUE COLLEGE BELIEF × IMPORTANCE = ATTRACTIVENESS	LOCAL STATE COLLEGE BELIEF × IMPORTANCE = ATTRACTIVENESS	WEST COAST UNIVERSITY BELIEF × IMPORTANCE = ATTRACTIVENESS
1. Learn a lot	.8 × 4 = 3.2	.9 × 4 = 3.6	.4 × 4 = 1.6	.8 × 4 = 3.2
2. Low cost	.6 × 2 = 1.2	0 × 2 = 0	1.0 × 2 = 2.0	.2 × 2 = .4
3. Good job	.7 × 5 = 3.5	1.0 × 5 = 5.0	.3 × 5 = 1.5	.7 × 5 = 3.5
4. Flexible program	.7 × 1 = .7	.7 × 1 = .7	.7 × 1 = .7	.7 × 1 = .7
5. Desirable location	.4 × 3 = 1.2	.7 × 3 = 2.1	.4 × 3 = 1.2	.9 × 3 = 2.7
Total attractiveness	9.8	11.4	7.0	10.5

Calculating the total amount of motivation to apply to each college

SCHOOL	MOTIVATIONAL COMPONENTS			TOTAL MOTIVATION
	TOTAL ATTRACTIVENESS OF COLLEGE	EXPECTANCY OF ADMITTANCE		
Big Ten university	9.8	×	.8 =	7.64
Ivy League college	11.4	×	.2 =	2.28
Local state college	7.0	×	1.0 =	7.0
West coast university	10.5	×	.6 =	6.3

That is, no *minimum level* of motivation has been specified in expectancy theory.

If the total motivational score had been zero, then expectancy theory predicts Bob will definitely *not* apply. The theory, thus, makes predictions at both extremes. That is, any school with a zero score will not be applied to and the one with the highest score will receive an application. However, expectancy theory does not specify *which* of the in-between schools will receive applications.

Expectancy theory also specifies how Bob will make his *final choice* after knowing which schools will accept him. The final choice, of course, depends on which schools actually accept Bob. If only one does so, there is no choice to be made. If two or more do so, the choice will be based on the *attractiveness* of each school. When a person has already been admitted, the expectancy factor is irrelevant. That is, expectancy = 1.0 for all those schools that accept Bob. Therefore, the differences among such schools are in terms of *attractiveness*.

One point should be remembered about expectancy theory as a model of organizational choice. The theory does *not* say that individuals actually write down all the information contained in Table 4.1, nor does it say individuals actually write out the calculations shown in Table 4.2. Expectancy theory *does* say that this is the way most people make decisions, whether or not they are consciously aware that all these factors are taken into account as stipulated in the model.

Using the situation in which Bob was participating in a research study was merely a literary convenience so that the various pieces of information could be presented in detailed form. Those who have criticized expectancy theory as being too rational prefer the *unprogrammed* view of decision making to be examined in the second case study. Their argument is that researchers who use questionnaires artificially create the appearance of rationality by forcing participants, such as Bob, into answering according to the prearranged format required by the expectancy theory model of decision making. Those who believe the unprogrammed view is more accurate than expectancy theory tend to avoid the use of structured questionnaires in favor of open-ended interviews with job candidates. It will be seen later that this difference in procedure for data gathering is important, because the two methods are extremely hard to compare.

Organizational Choice as an "Unprogrammed" Decision

The procedure just described can be thought of as a rather highly "programmed" approach to decision making. It is programmed in the sense that a number of factors were considered in the evaluation of different schools. Furthermore, each factor was given only as much "weight" as justified by its *importance* to the person making the choice. By way of contrast with Bob's systematic (and programmed) process, let's now consider the case of another college senior in a similar situation. Greg was also a senior at the same Big Ten university as Bob, but they were not acquainted. Greg's decision process was quite different—it was an *un*programmed approach to organizational choice.

Rather than considering five factors,[1] as Bob had, Greg was primarily concerned with only two, but very *crucial,* outcomes: (1) the prospects for a job upon graduation, and (2) the geographical location of the school. Regarding the first factor, Greg wanted to go to a high-prestige school. This seemed to him to be the best route to getting a job with a large, multinational corporation. For the second factor, Greg wanted to move from the midwest either to the west coast or to the New York City area. These two factors were absolute; i.e., Greg would not consider a high-prestige school in another area, nor would he consider a weak school in one of the desirable areas. These two criteria severely limited the scope of Greg's search for the ideal MBA program.

The schools that Greg labeled as "attractive" were thus selected via a different psychological process from the one that Bob used. First, *fewer criteria* were used to judge each school. Second, *the factors were not weighted by importance*—they were either *crucial* or practically irrelevant. There was less room for compromise in Greg's search than there was in Bob's search.

There were some similarities, however, between Bob's systematic approach and Greg's unprogrammed procedure. First, both men could give a fairly clear description of the ideal school, even though their *process* of coming to this decision differed. Second, both men *believed* they were being rational about the decision.

Bob and Greg also differed in making the decision to apply to schools. Bob considered four schools simultaneously and rated each in terms of the

---

[1] This is a good example of the difference between the two views. The unprogrammed view holds that Bob only considered five factors because he was asked to do so.

expectancy of being admitted. Greg's process was much less systematic. Rather than considering a number of schools, Greg began with his ideal choice. He appraised his chances for a successful admission. He then considered another highly attractive school in comparison with the ideal choice. Greg found it easier to make direct comparisons between two schools at a time, rather than to make the many subjective evaluations Bob made. Rarely did Greg consider (in an *active* way) more than two or (possibly) three schools. The total number of schools considered by Greg was actually larger than that considered by Bob, but the schools were considered *sequentially* rather than simultaneously.

The unprogrammed approach taken by Greg is also different from the expectancy theory model in its explanation of how individuals make the "final" choice. Bob chose the school that was the one highest in *attractiveness* of those that had accepted him. Bob's final choice was, then, based on a careful consideration of several factors, each of which was weighted by its importance.

In contrast, the unprogrammed approach taken by Greg was actually a two-stage process. The first stage was the development of an implicit choice (Soelberg 1967) of which Greg was not fully aware. In fact, the view of unprogrammed organizational choice stipulates that most individuals are not aware of the direction toward which they are actually leaning. Oftentimes it takes the "prodding" of another person to help the individual realize that he or she has already made an implicit decision. The implicit choice is usually based on only a few factors that are not weighted by importance as they are in expectancy theory.

The second stage is called *confirmation* (Soelberg 1967) and means the type of thinking used to *justify* one's implicit choice. In this stage there is a great deal of similarity between expectancy theory and the unprogrammed view. During confirmation the alternative organizations are compared across a much wider spectrum of factors, *and* the factors are weighted by their importance to the individual. However, the crucial difference is that the unprogrammed view stipulates that this occurs only *after* an individual has already made the decision. In contrast, expectancy theory says that this is how the decision was made in the first place.

The final difference between the two views of organizational choice is that the unprogrammed view says that individuals tend to *distort* both their perceptions about organizations *and* the importance they attach to various factors used to make the decision. This distortion is supposed to be a necessary step in the justification, or rationalization, of one's implicit choice. Other research in social psychology (Aronson 1972) supports this view that people rationalize choices *after* making them. This stems from a common human need to feel that one makes good choices. In this sense it has been said that most people need to *"feel* right" rather than to actually "be right" (Aronson 1972). In contrast, expectancy theory does not say whether or not distortion occurs.

EVALUATING THE TWO VIEWS OF ORGANIZATIONAL CHOICE

There are two questions to answer in comparing these two case studies of organizational choice. (1) Which of the two better represents the typical person? (2) Which is *better* for the welfare both of individuals and organizations? The first question can be discussed by referring to research studies. The second refers to which type of choice process will produce better long-term matches between individual and organization.

Research on organizational choice. While thousands of studies have been conducted on how occupational choices are made (Crites 1969), fewer than 20 studies have focused on *organizational* choices.

Expectancy theory stipulates how the *attractiveness* of an organization is determined, how much *effort to join* is expended, and how the *final choice* is made. In order to evaluate all three aspects of expectancy theory, it is necessary to obtain systematic data from job seekers over a period of time.

The *attractiveness* of an organization is supposed to be the result of *multiplying* one's *beliefs* about expected outcomes by the *importance* of those beliefs. (See Table 4.2.) Four studies examined this aspect of the organizational choice model. In the first of these (Sheard 1970), expectancy theory was supported, but the results were not strong. In the second (Lawler et al. 1975), the data do not appear to support the multiplicative aspect of expectancy theory. In the third one (Connolly and Vines 1977) expectancy theory was supported. Finally, the most recent study (Wanous, Keon, and Latack 1979) found the strongest support for this multiplicative combination, as specified by expectancy theory.

The amount of *effort* to enter an organization is supposed to be the result of a *multiplication* between *attractiveness* and the *expectancy* theory. The first study (Lawler et al., 1975) did not support the theory.

The second (Oldham 1976) found strong results supporting this multiplication of factors as the best way to represent the total effort to join an organization. In the most recent study (Wanous, Keon, and Latack 1979), support was again found. For example, the correlation between attractiveness (alone) and effort was .52, but expectancy $\times$ attractiveness correlated .71 with the amount of effort expended in applying to a particular graduate business school.

According to expectancy theory, one's *final choice* of an organization should be the one highest in *attractiveness* of those offering entry. Seven studies assessed how often the most attractive organization was actually chosen—a type of "hit rate." The results strongly support expectancy theory. In fact, this aspect of the model is most consistent with the research which has been conducted. The various hit rates for *attractiveness* predicting one's *final choice* are

- *80 percent based on attractiveness data gathered six months prior to final choice of which accounting firm to enter (Lawler et al. 1975).*
- *54 percent based on attractiveness data gathered several months prior to final choice of which college sorority to join (Oldham 1976).*
- *81 percent based on attractiveness data gathered after actually making the final choice to work for the Corning Glass Company (Pieters, Hundert, and Beer 1968).*
- *68 percent based on attractiveness data gathered after actually making the final choice of organization (Connolly and Vines 1977).*
- *68 percent based on attractiveness data gathered after naval officers had already chosen whether or not to retire (Parker and Dyer 1976).*
- *87 percent based on attractiveness data gathered before M.I.T. graduates took positions in business (Soelberg 1967).*
- *76 percent based on attractiveness data gathered a few months before Carnegie—Mellon MBAs took jobs in industry (Vroom 1966).*

In sum, expectancy theory seems to be a good way to describe organizational choices, but not nearly enough research has been done to call those results conclusive. (See Wanous 1977; Wanous, Keon, and Latack 1979 for more details about these studies.)

Research into the unprogrammed view is also scarce. It is difficult to assess this model because it is less specific than expectancy theory. Therefore, it is difficult to evaluate the results of the studies done on it.

Three investigations of the unprogrammed model have been reported. The first of these (Soelberg 1967) found that 74 percent of the people studied could identify an "acceptable choice" two weeks *prior* to the end of their search for job offers. Soelberg considered that this finding supported the unprogrammed view. Expectancy theory stipulates that one's organizational choice is made *after* all relevant information has been collected, not *prior* to it as found by Soelberg.

Two subsequent studies, inspired by Soelberg's original investigation, did *not* find the same degree of "irrational" behavior (Glueck 1974; Sheridan, Richards, and Slocum 1975). For example, 47 percent of the subjects in one study could *not* specify a set of "necessary and sufficient" outcomes that would govern their search for acceptable jobs (Sheridan et al. 1975). Thus the unprogrammed model does not seem to be typical, although it probably is accurate for a minority of people.

Should individuals make rational career and organizational choices? What the typical person does is not the same as what the typical person *should* have done. The data on how organizational choices are made support the rational approach of expectancy theory as the more typical. Yet not everyone is this rational. Some individuals make choices in ways that do *not* involve the search for lots of information and the careful consideration of each alternative. According to the Matching Model, this leads to less than maximum satisfaction with one's choice of organization. The data in Chapter 2 on the "falling satisfaction" of newcomers certainly confirm this.

In the area of *occupational* choices, a step-by-step procedure has been developed to help people think more clearly and systematically about career choices (Janis and Wheeler 1978). The procedure seems easily transferable to organizational choices.

Janis and Wheeler (1978) have developed the "decision counselor" approach to career decision making. Their efforts have been directed toward this development because they felt that career choices are hard to reverse if they turn out to be wrong.

The main thrust of the decision counselor approach is to have individuals identify all the relevant alternatives and then carefully evaluate each one according to the "balance sheet" approach. Table 4.3 shows an example. Four categories are included: (1) tangible gains and losses for self, (2) tangible gains and losses for others, (3) self-approval or self-disapproval, and (4) social approval or disapproval.

Why all the fuss about helping people behave more rationally? Janis and Mann (1977) identified four ways people cope with tough decisions (particularly those in their personal lives: (1) complacency, (2) defensive avoidance, (3) hypervigilance, and (4) vigilance. Only the last "coping style" is rational in the expectancy theory sense. *Complacency* is the coping style used by those who ignore negative information. For example, a new Ph.D. may take a job in a small college rather than in a big university to "avoid the publish-or-perish rat race." The person is complacently assuming that job security will be greater in the small college, but the facts may not support this assumption.

Defensive avoidance is a type of denial of the risks involved in making career or organizational choices. People who are defensively avoiding the facts concerning these choices are often quite calm in appearance. They are typically unaware of their defensiveness. There are, however, three tell-tale signs of this coping style. (1) Rationalization, "It can't happen to me."; (2) Procrastination, "Nothing needs to be done now. I can take care of it later."; and (3) Buck passing, "I'm not the one who needs to do it. Let someone else do it."

Hypervigilance is the coping style used by people who are faced with making a crucial choice under severe time pressure. An extreme form of hypervigilance is panic. The hypervigilant person does not consider a full range of options and may tend to select the first reasonable one that comes along. The person may even display visible signs of stress during the decision process. In a "tight" labor market, some college seniors become hypervigilant.

Vigilant decision making is employed by those who acknowledge there are risks involved in all choices, who believe there is a best solution, and who believe there is enough time to make a thoroughly systematic decision. Vigilant decision makers recognize risks and make contingency plans. In contrast, the other three types do not and are emotionally un-prepared even for minor setbacks. The balance sheet procedure (Table 4.3) is extremely useful in focusing on the facts of each alternative career or organizational choice. Janis and Wheeler (1978) report that the decision balance sheet was quite well received in four experiments: (1) with Yale seniors deciding what to do the next year, (2) with high school seniors deciding whether or not to attend college, (3) with adults deciding whether or not to diet, and (4) with adults deciding whether to attend an early morning exercise class for health reasons.

TABLE 4.3

A manager's balance sheet

The grid lays out the pros and cons of one alternative facing a production manager at a large manufacturing plant who is contemplating a job change: whether or not to remain in the present position. Balance sheets would be filled out as well for all other alternatives—for example, whether to seek a lateral transfer within the company.

	POSITIVE ANTICIPATIONS	NEGATIVE ANTICIPATIONS
Tangible gains and losses for self	1. Satisfactory pay	1. Long hours
	2. Plenty of opportunities to use my skills and competencies	2. Constant time pressures—deadlines too short
	3. For the present, my status in organization is OK (but it won't be for long if I am not promoted in the next year)	3. Unpleasant paperwork
		4. Poor prospects for advancement to a higher-level position
		5. Repeated reorganizations make my work chaotic
		6. Constant disruption from high turnover of other executives I deal with
Tangible gains and losses for others	1. Adequate income for family	1. Not enough time free to spend with my family
	2. Spouse and children get special privileges because of my position in the firm	2. Spouse often has to put up with my irritability when I come home after bad days at work

Self-approval or self-disapproval	
1. This position allows me to make full use of my potentialities	1. Sometimes feel I'm a fool to continue putting up with the unreasonable deadlines and other stupid demands made by the top managers
2. Proud of my achievements	
3. Proud of the competent team I have shaped up	
4. Sense of meaningful accomplishment when I see the products for which we are responsible	

Social approval or disapproval	
1. Approval of men on my team, who look up to me as their leader and who are good friends	1. Very slight skeptical reaction of my spouse who asks me if I might be better off in a different firm
2. Approval of my superior who is a friend and wants me to stay	2. A friend in another firm who has been wanting to wangle something for me will be disappointed

Source: I. Janis and D. Wheeler, 1978. Thinking clearly about career choices. *Psychology Today* (May): 75. Reprinted from *Psychology Today* Magazine. Copyright © 1978 by Ziff-Davis Publishing Company.

Besides the balance sheet technique, *stress inoculation* is used *after* the decision, but before it is carried out. This is almost exactly the same as realistic recruitment except that Janis believes it is appropriate only *after* a choice (Janis and Mann 1977; Janis and Wheeler 1978). The position throughout this book has been that realistic information is also a very valuable input to the decision itself, even though it's not always possible to provide realistic information prior to organizational choice.

The best example of stress inoculation is Janis's own work with patients in hospitals (Janis and Mann 1977) that was mentioned in Chapter 3. In these situations the patients in the various studies had all decided to have operations, but had not gone through the surgery when specially trained nurses gave them the stress inoculation. The inoculation was designed to deflate unrealistically positive views about the hospital stay, but did not go so far as to terrify the patient. This postdecision, preimplementation form of realistic preview was reportedly successful in helping patients during the postoperative period.

The final technique used to promote vigilant decision making is called *outcome psychodrama*—a type of role-playing exercise. The decision counselor asks the client to assume that a particular career (or organization) has already been chosen, and to reflect on what has happened since making the choice (Janis and Wheeler 1978). The client is asked to repeat and expand upon the scenario until all the potential risks and benefits are considered. The decision counselor keeps a "low profile," relying instead on the client to generate the list of consequences associated with each alternative. Janis and Wheeler report only limited use of outcome psychodrama. Therefore, its effectiveness at the present is unknown. They do caution that a particularly intense session may backfire causing feelings of hopelessness—just the type of defensive avoidance that one is trying to overcome with this approach.

REDUCING THE NUMBER OF "BACK-OUTS" FROM AN ORGANIZATIONAL CHOICE

Up to now the entry process has appeared to be a pretty straightforward process. In fact, however, people often change their minds and back out of an organizational choice. In fact some firms have experienced backout rates as high as 15 percent of the commitments made by job candidates. From the organization's viewpoint, this is an undesirable situation.

One study of the back-out problem used the straightforward principle of positive reinforcement to tackle this problem (Ivancevich and Donnelly 1971). The researchers found two organizations willing to try an experiment in which half of those accepting a job offer were called on the phone three times, while the other half were not called at all (but continued to receive company literature). It was expected that this reinforcement would reduce the number of back-outs—*and it did*. In one company the percentage of back-outs was only 2.2 percent in the experimental group versus 10.8 percent in the group handled in the usual way. In the other company the percentages were 2.9 percent versus 10.7 percent. From an organizational entry viewpoint, it is unfortunate that the newcomers were not subsequently studied to see what effect this treatment would have later on.

RELATIONSHIP OF ORGANIZATIONAL CHOICE TO RECRUITMENT

In the two preceding chapters, much was said about the extensive problems related to the inflated expectations held by job candidates as outsiders to organizations. After reading the two accounts of organizational choice, it should be clear that *both* views of the choice process depend heavily on the beliefs and expectations of individuals. The dependence on expectations is probably greater for the expectancy theory model of organizational choice, but the unprogrammed view also contains similar components. In expectancy theory the accuracy of information obtained by outsiders affects (1) their beliefs about what the organization has to offer and (2) their *expectations* of gaining entry if they apply.

Despite all that was said in Chapters 2 and 3, relatively little mention was made of inflated expectations in this chapter. The question may have occurred to the reader whether this was an oversight, or whether inflated expectations completely undercut any systematic theory of organizational choice. It may be wondered how expectancy theory could be used as a model of organizational choice when it has already been established that outsider expectations are often incorrectly inflated. This is *not* as serious a problem as it might appear to be. In fact, there is *no* inconsistency between the theme of Chapters 2 and 3, and the present one.

The key to understanding the relationship between recruitment and organizational choice is to remember that individuals make choices as

outsiders, prior to discovering that some of their beliefs were grossly inflated. At the time most organizational choices are made, outsiders are
unaware of organizational realities; i.e., they tend to hold "naive" expectations (Wanous 1976). Thus it is possible for individuals to act in the way
expectancy theory (or the unprogrammed view) predicts they will. The
long-range wisdom of organizational choices made with realistic expectations is greater than those decisions made on much less information because people are better able to match their own needs to an appropriate
organizational climate. However, the process of making the choice is
similar in both cases, even if the consequences are not.

ORGANIZATIONAL CHOICE AND THE INTERVIEW

The interview is used in almost all organizations. As with the other events
of organizational entry, the interview can be analyzed both from an individual and an organizational viewpoint. This is because it fulfills two functions during entry—recruitment and selection. Since the focus here is on
organizational choice, this section will examine two aspects concerning the
recruitment function. First, the impact of an interview on how individuals
choose organizations is discussed. Second, the results of research studies
on the interpersonal dynamics of the interview are interpreted so that
advice can be given to job candidates about to be interviewed for employment. The role of the interview as a selection mechanism is discussed in
Chapter 5.

How the Interview Affects an Individual's Organizational Choice

Although most people recognize that an employment interview has a recruitment function as well as a selection function, relatively little research
has been done that concerns the recruitment aspect. Instead, most of the
research efforts have been aimed at the interviewer, rather than at the job
candidate. This should not be surprising. This book has emphasized the
lack of attention paid to the individual's view of organizational entry.

Two recent studies have been directed at interviewee reactions. One
was done at Cornell University of 112 first- and second-year MBA students
(Alderfer and McCord 1970). The first-year students were seeking summer
employment. The second-year students were graduating and looking for
full-time jobs. The other study was done at Michigan State University of

237 undergraduates (Schmitt and Coyle 1976). Again some of the under-graduates were seeking summer jobs and others full-time positions.

The Cornell study addressed the question of how an interview affects the organizational choices made by individuals. The students were asked to think about three interviews: the best, the worst, and the average one. For each of these three they were then asked to describe their reactions on a questionnaire. Among the questions asked were two directly relevant for the model of organization choice used here. The first one asked the job candidates to rate their "chances for a job offer," and the second one asked them to rate "how likely they were to accept an offer if one were given."

Students who were asked about the *best* interview said there was a 60 percent chance they would accept a job offer. When asked about their reaction to the *average* interview, the chances fell to 35 percent. Finally, for the *worst* interviews students said there was only a 17 percent chance they would take a job with that organization.

These results clearly show that an individual's reaction to the interview affects the job candidate significantly and has important implications for the *recruitment* function of the interview. If individuals get "turned off" at the initial contact with a company, they are much less likely to continue seeking employment there.

The next logical question to ask is what factors cause people to be satisfied with employment interviews. Both the Cornell and the Michigan State studies dealt with this question. The Cornell Study divided these factors into three groups: (1) interviewer behavior, (2) attitude of inter-viewer, and (3) attitudes of the job candidates themselves. The *behaviors* of an interviewer that enhanced the attractiveness of the experience for candidates were as follows: answered questions, told about careers of other MBA graduates, asked the candidate to discuss his or her strengths and weaknesses, asked a technical question, indicated a high salary might be possible, and showed familiarity with the applicant's background. The *attitudes* of interviewers which led to satisfactory experiences were: seemed interested in the candidate, understood the viewpoint of an MBA, and seemed interested in what the individual could contribute. Finally, the *attitudes* of the *candidates* that led to their being satisfied with the interview were: being interested in getting a job offer, and feeling that he or she could handle all questions asked by the interviewer.

In the Michigan State study of job candidate reactions, a total of 74 questions was grouped into six general categories, based on statistical analysis. This was done so that it would be easier to discuss the basic trends occurring during the interviews. The six factors were: the interviewer was a "nice person," how the interview was conducted, the perceived aggressiveness of the interviewer, the degree to which the interviewer was correct or well informed, the amount of specific job information given, and how interested the interviewer seemed to be in the candidate. Of all these factors, the "nice person" impression was the most important. The perception of an interviewer as a nice, likeable person included such specific factors as dependability, thoughtfulness, cooperativeness, warmth, and perceptiveness.

Coping with the Employment Interview

Much of the research on interviews has focused on how the interviewer makes decisions about job candidates. As an outgrowth of this research, there are some results relevant for job candidates. (See Mayfield 1964; Ulrich and Trumbo 1965; Wagner 1949; and Wright 1969 for early reviews, and Schmitt 1976; and Osburn and Constantin 1977 for more recent review articles.) Selected conclusions from research on employment interviews are presented in the context of what they mean for the job candidate.

Initial impressions are crucial. Most studies of interviews indicate that the *order* in which information is presented to the interviewer is a highly significant factor. The information obtained *first* has a more significant impact on the decision to hire than that gathered later in the interview. This has been called the "primacy effect," in contrast to the "recency effect." A dramatic example of the primacy effect was revealed in a study that found that the average interviewer reached a conclusion about job candidates after only four minutes of a 15-minute interview (Springbett 1958).

This research finding is important because behavioral scientists have studied the order in which information is presented in a wide variety of situations, e.g., political campaigns and legal proceedings. The primacy effect does *not* occur universally, but it does seem to occur in job interviews. The only time recency effects are found is in the situation in which interviewers are asked to make *two* ratings of candidates, i.e., an initial one and a final one. In this particular situation the information uncovered last has the greater influence on the hiring decision (Osburn and Constantin 1977).

The best explanation for the dominance of early information is that the attention of the interviewer decreases over time. This explains why primacy effects occur with only one rating. It also explains why recency effects occur with repeated ratings because the attention of the interviewer is aroused by having to complete a second formal evaluation. The situation of repeated ratings is typically found in tightly monitored research studies. Outside the context of a research study, however, the interviewer generally makes just one evaluation that is heavily influenced by *initial* impressions and information.

What this means to the job candidate is quite clear. First impressions *do* count heavily. Job candidates are often advised to be "on time" and to "dress appropriately" (Adams 1977). This advice is usually considered so obvious that no proof is generally offered to substantiate it. However, it must be remembered that two of the earliest pieces of information the interviewer gathers concern the punctuality and physical appearance of job candidates.

Negative information is given high significance. The importance of this research finding is obvious. One study found that a *single* piece of negative information led to a 90 percent chance of a rejection (Springbett 1958). Virtually all research studies of job interviews show that negative information is given a much higher weight relative to positive information by the interviewers. One or two negatives can far outweigh a much larger number of positive factors. Thus the advice to job candidates is clear; interviewers tend to look for information that leads to a rejection rather than to a selection.

Psychologists have spent quite a lot of time trying to understand the reasons why negative information outweighs the positive. At least four have been uncovered. First, most interviewers reflect a corporate strategy of being cost oriented. In most cases it is true that hiring an incompetent person costs more than do the lost opportunities of passing over a qualified person. Therefore, most interviewers try to avoid costly mistakes in hiring, even though they realize an occasional "gem" may be lost. A second reason is that some jobs are easily performed by a large percentage of those interviewed. Thus the interviewer needs to find some way to reject candidates, hence even a "small" negative fact can lead to rejection of a job candidate.

A third reason stems from a "figure-ground" contrast. Think of the following situation. A tall tree seems to "stand out" among a much larger cluster of shorter trees. In this case the tall tree is the "figure" and the others form the "ground" (or background). The typical interview presents a similar situation. When the majority of information is positive, a small number of negatives easily diverts the attention of an interviewer. The fourth and final reason is that interviewers are typically more familiar with failures than successes. This is because they are quite likely to be criticized for unsuccessful hires, since they contributed to the decision. Thus interviewers tend to know more specifics about who failed than they do about who succeeded.

Other ways to cope. The importance of the primacy effect during the interview and the role of negative information are firmly grounded in research. Other research conclusions regarding the interview will be reserved for Chapter 5 on selection because they are of more concern for the organization conducting interviews than for job candidates.

Knowing what types of questions to expect may be helpful to job candidates. The questions usually fall into four categories: (1) open-ended, (2) hypothetical situation, (3) specific, and (4) stress. The last type is not nearly as popular today as it once was (Adams 1974). Examples of the open-ended question include: "Where do you see yourself in five years?", "How did you select your educational program?", or "What's your strategy for job search?" The hypothetical business situation is a favorite question, but may assume too much job experience in the case of students graduating from school. In such cases a variation is to inquire about personal interests and then use follow-up questions to learn about how the individual approaches decisions or problems. Finally, specific questions may be asked of the candidate about technical areas that the person presumably has learned about through education or work experience. The job candidate who can answer these questions *and* who can also *ask* specific questions about the organization will get higher ratings. Asking questions of your own is usually taken as an indicator of high motivation by most recruiters (Adams 1974).

CHOOSING TO LEAVE AN ORGANIZATION

Is there any reason to suppose that the decision to leave is much different from the decision to join? Insiders who decide to quit typically consider factors *different* from the factors considered by those who join. The position taken here is that the two decisions *are* nearly identical in terms of the *process* followed, however. The *expectancy theory* way of organizing information, highlighted in the case study of Bob earlier in this chapter, is just as useful in understanding how insiders decide to quit as it is in describing how outsiders decide to join.

Despite the simplicity of this approach, the study of turnover in organizations has had a curious history. Over 20 years ago, March and Simon (1958) spelled out a detailed model of the "decision to participate" in an organization. Yet, many researchers ignored this model and studied all the possible factors (both individual characteristics and situational factors) that might in some way be related to turnover. The outcome of this voluminous body of research has been that some type of category system is necessary to organize all the findings. This has meant that those attempting to draw general conclusions from turnover research often used *different* category systems from each other. This has had the effect of complicating any concise knowledge about decisions to leave organizations.

Over the years, a number of literature reviews concerning turnover have been done (Brayfield and Crockett 1955; Forrest, Cummings, and Johnson 1977; Herzberg, Mausner, Peterson, and Capwell 1957; Mobley, Griffeth, Hand, and Meglino 1979; Price 1977; Porter and Steers 1973; Schuh 1967; and Vroom 1964). Despite the many efforts to study the reasons why individuals leave organizations, relatively little can be learned from the compilation of results as seen in these many reviews. The major reason for this extreme skepticism about previous turnover research is that almost all studies have been flawed in one of these ways.

1. In too many cases, voluntary versus involuntary turnover have not been separated. The Matching Model clearly indicates that each type of turnover is likely to be caused by *different* factors. That is, low job performance should result in being fired, whereas low job satisfaction should result in one's quitting.

2. The length of one's tenure in an organization is rarely taken into consideration. Yet, we know that the longer individuals remain within an organization, the less likely they are to quit. Without careful consideration of this factor, it is impossible to make fair comparisons among different studies.

3. Far too few studies have been guided by a theory. Instead, some researchers have chosen to study whatever data happen to be conveniently

available. This makes it hard to compare the results of different studies because different factors are measured and evaluated.

4. Many studies have examined turnover in relationship to other factors one at a time, rather than considering the impact of a *set* of factors on turnover. As an example, consider age and the length of one's tenure in an organization. Both of these have been consistently related to turnover (see Table 4.4). However, we also know that age and tenure are related to each other; i.e., someone with 30 years of tenure is probably at least 50 years old. The statistical disentangling of these two factors is possible, but sufficiently difficult that it has not been done frequently.

Model of voluntary turnover. Figure 4.3 is an expanded version of the Matching Model. It focuses on the individual's decision to leave an organization. There are two additions in Fig. 4.3: (1) a "comparison of one's present job to other alternatives," and (2) "actions to secure another job."

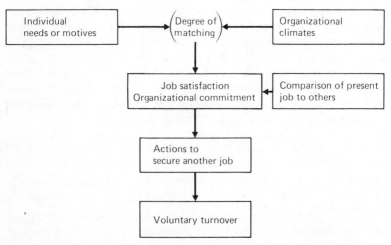

Fig 4.3 *Expanded model of voluntary turnover.*

In the original version of the Matching Model used throughout this book, the degree of which an individual's needs "matched" the needs reinforcement from organizational climates determined the level of one's job satisfaction. In the expanded version, however, the focus is enlarged to include a comparison of one's presently held job with other job possibilities. Neither individuals, nor organizations, exist in a vacuum. The degree of one's job satisfaction is certainly influenced by such a comparison (Wanous and Lawler 1972). In fact, comparison processes are well grounded in psychology, e.g., as in social comparison theory (Festinger 1954) or in equity theory (Adams 1963).[2]

The comparison process can be directly linked to the expectancy theory model of organizational choice, thereby demonstrating that the same process operates for *both* organizational entry *and* exit. By this is meant that *two* factors combine to yield overall job satisfaction: (1) an individual's *beliefs* about what rewards are obtained from organizational climates, and (2) the *importance* of each reward to the person. Thus the determination of job satisfaction is identical to the way in which organizational *attractiveness* is obtained (see Table 4.2). (Job satisfaction does *not* contain an expectancy factor because it refers to people already inside an organization. That is, Expectancy = 1.00 for those already on the inside.)

The comparison of one's present job with other possibilities involves *two* types of comparison: (1) with the *attractiveness* of other organizations, and (2) with the *total motivation* to join another organization. (See Table 4.2 for the way these are derived.) Several possibilities may result from such comparisons:

1. Present job satisfaction is *greater* than the attractiveness of other jobs. (In this case, the individual will report high job satisfaction and will make little or no effort to leave the organization.)

2. Present job satisfaction is *less* than the attractiveness of an alternative job, but is *greater* than the total motivation to join the alternative. (In this case, it is likely that the individual will be somewhat dissatisfied, but will not make serious attempts to leave. A person like this could be "looking" most of the time. It is also possible that such a person has already looked around and knows that attractive alternatives will not offer admittance at the present time.)

3. Present job satisfaction is *less* than the total motivation to join an alternative organization. (In this case, low job satisfaction is translated into specific actions designed to leave for the alternative. Individuals in this situation are "on the way out.")

---

[2] Discussion of social comparison and equity theories is beyond the scope of this book.

TABLE 4.4

Summary of three reviews of the turnover literature

VARIABLE	PORTER AND STEERS (1973)	PRICE (1977)	MOBLEY ET AL. (1979)
Personal characteristic			
Age	Consistent negative	Consistent negative	Consistent negative
Tenure	Consistent negative	Consistent negative	Consistent negative
Similarity of job with vocational interests	Weak negative		
Personality	Weak negative for extreme traits		
Family size and responsibilities	Generally positive for women; inconclusive for males		
Sex		Inconclusive	Inconclusive
Education		Weak positive	Inconclusive
Weighted application blank			Moderate positive
Overall job satisfaction	Consistent negative	Consistent negative	Consistent negative
Organizational and job characteristic			
Pay	Consistent negative	Consistent negative	Inconclusive
Promotion	Consistent negative	Weak negative	Inconclusive
Size of organization	Inconclusive	Inconclusive	
Size of work unit	Consistent positive for blue collar; inconclusive for white collar	Inconclusive	
Peer group interaction	Moderate negative		Inconclusive
Integration		Consistent negative	
Supervision style	Consistent negative	Consistent negative	Moderate negative
Instrumental communication		Consistent negative	

Variable		
Formal communication		Consistent negative
Role clarity	Consistent negative	
Job autonomy and responsibility	Consistent negative	
Centralization	Moderate positive	Consistent negative
Task repetitiveness		Weak positive
Overall reaction to job content	Consistent negative	Consistent negative
Occupational grouping		
Blue collar; skilled vs. unskilled		Moderate (unskilled higher)
Blue collar vs. white collar		Moderate (blue collar higher)
Nonmanagers vs. managers		Weak (nonmanagers higher)
Nongovernment vs. government		Weak (nongovernment higher)
Professionalism		Weak positive (professionalism higher)
External environment		
Level of employment/opportunity	Consistent positive	Consistent positive
Perceived alternatives		Weak positive
Recently studied variable		
Intentions to quit		Consistent positive
Commitment/attachment		Consistent negative
Met expectations		Weak negative

Source: Mobley et al., 1979. Review and conceptual analysis of the employee turnover process. *Psychological Bulletin* **86**: 514–515. Reprinted by permission.

Factors related to turnover. The model in Fig. 4.3 shows the *psychological process* used in deciding to leave or stay in an organization. It does not, however, show *which factors* (individual *and* organizational characteristics) seem to cause low job satisfaction. Much research has been done to identify the "turnover prone" person, as well as that directed at organizational conditions that typically cause high turnover. In fact, the vast majority of research on turnover has been directed toward the identification of these factors, rather than toward an attempt to validate a theoretical model of the process itself.

The three most comprehensive and recent reviews of the literature on turnover are compared in Table 4.4 (Porter and Steers 1973; Price 1977; Mobley et al. 1979). In the table, the term "negative" means that the greater the value of one factor, the lower the turnover rate. For example, the greater one's job satisfaction, the lower the turnover.

For the most part, there is agreement among the three reviews in the conclusions drawn. The most recent review (Mobley et al., 1979) covered only 1973–1978. The other two covered studies done in the 1950s and 1960s (and a few in the early 1970s). The only area of major disagreement between the most recent review and the two earlier ones was found in the area of pay and promotions. The earlier reviews found that the higher the pay and the greater the chances for a promotion, the lower the turnover. The review of recent studies found no such trend.

An example of a "large" turnover study. Earlier, most studies of turnover were criticized for five reasons. In this section, a recent study (Wanous, Stumpf, and Bedrosian 1979) will be described to indicate what happens when a systematic approach is taken to studying why individuals leave organizations.

This study was conducted in cooperation with the New York State Department of Employment Service. All of those placed on jobs through this state agency in a one-month period ($N = 2,268$ persons) were monitored for the first 28 weeks on the new job. Of this number, 1,736 were included for final statistical analysis because not everyone responded to the questionnaire survey of both employers and employees. During the 28-week period, 632 voluntarily left their jobs, 607 were involuntarily separated (includes firing, as well as companies that moved or folded), and 497 remained employed.

This study is noteworthy because voluntary and involuntary turnover were considered separately, consistent with the Matching Model. The length of tenure in the organization was not confounded in the results, since all participants were newly hired. A large number of individual differences and organizational factors were considered as possible causes of turnover. These factors were themselves arranged in a logical, causal sequence based on theory derived from the Matching Model. Finally, the 1,736 persons were employed in a wide variety of organizations throughout New York State. Thus there was a large sample of *both* individuals *and* organizations. Figure 4.4 shows how the various factors were arranged for the statistical analysis.

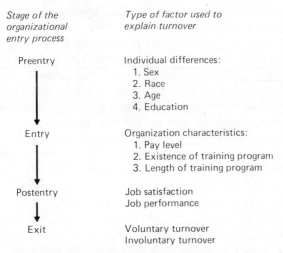

Stage of the organizational entry process	*Type of factor used to explain turnover*
Preentry	Individual differences: 1. Sex 2. Race 3. Age 4. Education
Entry	Organization characteristics: 1. Pay level 2. Existence of training program 3. Length of training program
Postentry	Job satisfaction Job performance
Exit	Voluntary turnover Involuntary turnover

Fig. 4.4 *Explanatory factors in turnover as arranged by stage of organizational entry.*

Based on the Matching Model, the following predictions were made and tested:

1. Satisfaction and performance should have the most significant impact on turnover because they are the "closest" to turnover in the temporal sequence shown in Fig. 4.4. (*Confirmed* by the data).

2. The relationship between job performance and *in*voluntary turnover should be stronger than the relationship between job satisfaction and *in*voluntary turnover. (*Confirmed* by the data.)

3. Those who left *in*voluntarily should have lower performance ratings, on the average, than those who quit voluntarily. (*Confirmed* by the data.)

4. The relationship between job satisfaction and voluntary turnover should be stronger than the relationship between job performance and voluntary turnover. (*Not confirmed* by the data; they were equally related to voluntary turnover.)

5. The average job satisfaction of those who left voluntarily should be lower than those who left involuntarily. (*Confirmed* by the data.)

Besides these predictions based on the theory of the Matching Model, the impact of *both* individual differences and organizational characteristics on turnover was investigated. The results showed that the three organizational characteristics at the "entry" level (pay, training, and length of training) were all related to both types of turnover, but *less* strongly related than either satisfaction or performance. As an example, pay level was an important factor in predicting voluntary turnover, but less important in explaining involuntary turnover. Finally, the four "individual differences" were completely *un*related to either type of turnover.

Several conclusions can be drawn from this study of turnover. First, strong support was found for the Matching Model used throughout this book. Second, the "best" explanations of turnover are those "closest" to it in the causal sequence shown in Fig. 4.4. The more removed a factor is, the weaker is its relationship to turnover. Third, the lack of relationship between "individual differences" and turnover found in this study is somewhat different from the results of other ones (see Table 4.4). The best explanation is that this study included a *wide variety* of different organizations—it was *not* a study of a *single* organization. Therefore, it was possible to examine the differences *across* organizations (as in different pay levels and training programs).

CONCLUSIONS

1. Organizational choice is a more limited topic than is the vocational entry process. Organizational choices typically follow occupational choices and are usually easier to reverse.

2. Organizational choice has been described in two alternative ways: as a systematic, rational choice by expectancy theory and as an

unprogrammed decision. These two views differ in the amount of information considered in the decision, the number of criteria used, and in how individuals process the information that is obtained.

3. Both views of organizational choices have received some research support due to the different research designs used to study each one. More studies of expectancy theory have been done, and the evidence seems stronger in the case of expectancy theory than in the unprogrammed version of organizational choice.

4. Decision counseling is a new approach to help individuals be "vigilant" decision makers in a way similar to expectancy theory. Such counseling includes: balance sheets, stress inoculation, and outcome psychodrama.

5. The pervasive problem of incorrect (inflated) expectations does *not* directly affect the degree to which individuals try to be rational in making an organizational choice. However, the long-term wisdom of organizational choices is impaired by inflated expectations.

6. Job interviews have both a recruitment and selection function. The recruitment function has been largely ignored by researchers, but can significantly influence organizational choices.

7. The importance of first impressions in job interviews and the disproportionate weight given to negative information are the two most relevant facts for the job candidate to anticipate.

8. The choice to leave an organization can be described in the same way as the choice to enter one. The major difference between the two is in the larger amount and greater accuracy of information used in exit decisions.

9. Most research on turnover has been flawed in one or more ways.

10. The Matching Model is a good way to represent the factors causing both voluntary and involuntary turnover.

Selection of Newcomers
by an Organization

5

The volume of writing on organizational selection is rather large because organizational selection has been the major focus of industrial psychologists for over 60 years. Some have traced the historical roots of interest in selection back to the turn of the century (Korman 1977). The largest single factor early in the development of personnel selection was the outbreak of World War I that increased the need to "process" people entering the armed forces.

The objective of this chapter is to discuss the major components of selection without going into the technical detail of statistics, psychological measurement, and current legal guidelines. The chapter is divided into three topic areas: (1) an overview of the selection process; (2) how job candidates are assessed, which includes the topics of testing, interviewing and, in particular, the use of assessment centers; and (3) how the utility (i.e., costs in relation to benefits) of a particular selection procedure is determined.

Although this chapter is written from the organization's perspective— how to select newcomers—its major appeal may be in preparing job candidates for the process of being selected. This is because the field of personnel selection has become complicated in a legalistic as well as a technical statistical sense. Personnel officers must consult far more detailed sources on the various aspects of selection in today's legal climate. [See Arvey (1979) for an up-to-date treatment of selection techniques and legal technicalities.]

The theme of *realism,* a major component of earlier chapters, is also present in this treatment of selection. A very popular and useful approach to both hiring and promotion today is the *assessment center* method, briefly mentioned in the case study of Ed in Chapter 1. An assessment center can easily be thought of as "realistic selection" since the philosophy is to *simulate the key elements of the job in short exercises.* To the extent that companies are successful in "capturing" the critical behaviors necessary for job success, they present a realistic job preview to job candidates. This, however, is *not* the intended purpose of assessment centers. They are designed to *select* rather than to *recruit* newcomers. A major point of this book is that recruitment and selection cannot be so easily separated. Besides providing a pretty good way to make selection decisions, assessment centers also may provide a good way to recruit newcomers via the realistic expectations the centers create.

OVERVIEW OF SELECTION

The selection process is graphically depicted in Fig. 5.1. At the beginning of this sequence is *job analysis,* which is the name for a variety of activities concerned with analyzing *both* (1) the skills necessary to do a job, and (2) the typical rewards (financial, psychological, etc.) received by people on a job. Thus Step 1 is a crucial part of any selection procedure, and one that should be carefully done. The organization which does not have accurate information about the job has difficulty matching the newcomer to it.

Step 2 shows that twin processes occur. On the left side it is necessary to select criteria of job performance, i.e., what measures will be used to evaluate a person's performance on a particular job. This is a crucial early step because the organization must know the meaning of job success if competent newcomers are to be selected. (Actually, measures of job performance can be used for other personnel functions, e.g., giving promotions and raises, or deciding who needs further training and development. Since these latter uses do not directly deal with organizational entry, they are excluded.)

On the right side of Step 2 the organization must choose a selection procedure that accurately reflects the important aspects of the job. There should be a close correspondence between the types of criteria used to evaluate an insider's performance, and the procedures used to assess the potential of an outsider job candidate.

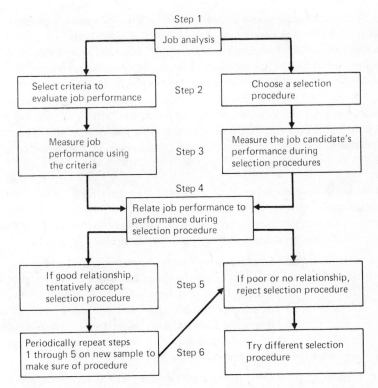

Fig. 5.1 *Outline of the organizational selection process. (Adapted from M. L. Blum and J. C. Naylor, 1968,* Industrial Psychology: Its Theoretical and Social Foundations, *p. 27. Copyright © 1968 by Milton L. Blum and James C. Naylor. Reprinted by permission of Harper & Row, Publishers, Inc.)*

Step 3 involves *measuring* (usually quantitatively) performance during selection and performance on the job. Step 4 is, then, the relationship between these two measures; it is commonly expressed as a *correlation*.[1] Step 5 is a decision to tentatively accept the selection procedure as *valid,*

[1] A correlation is an index number of how closely two factors are related to each other. A *zero* correlation means no relationship at all. A 1.00 correlation (the maximum) shows a perfectly positive relationship. A 1.00 correlation shows a perfectly negative relationship.

or to continue research on a better way to do it. The meaning of *test validity* and how it is determined is the subject of entire books [see, for example Arvey (1979)] because it involves both psychological and statistical definitions. Assessing the validity of a selection procedure is typically done by Ph.D. industrial psychologists who are competent in statistics.

Before moving to a discussion of how job candidates are assessed, the procedures for doing a job analysis and selecting criteria of job performance are highlighted. There are two necessary foundations to the actual appraising and selecting of newcomers, as shown in the sequence of Fig. 5.1.

How is job analysis information obtained? The assessment of jobs must use a variety of methods, as pointed out in Chapter 3 when diagnosis for realistic recruitment was covered. At least nine methods have been used to obtain information about jobs (Blum and Naylor 1968):

1. *Questionnaires.* Employees are asked to provide data about both themselves and the way they see their own job. There are several problems with this method. First, it is time consuming in terms of lost hours of work for which employees are paid. Second, it assumes a reasonably high degree of trust between lower level employees and management. Third, jobholders do not remember all events that compose a job. Fourth, writing skills vary from person to person.

2. *Checklist.* A variation of the questionnaire method asks employees to check off those job duties and characteristics that are relevant for the job performed. Generally speaking, they are a bit easier to fill out and tabulate, but still are affected by the same basic problems as are longer, more detailed questionnaires.

3. *Individual interview.* Usually a representative *sample* of employees from a particular job is interviewed because interviews are more time consuming than questionnaires. After the interviews, a narrative description is written by the job analyst.

4. *Observation interview.* A variation of the interview is to combine it with actual observation of the employee at work. This can produce more detailed results and greater insight into the nature of a job, but is even more time consuming than a straight interview. This is because the job analyst must remain on the job long enough to see the full range of duties that the employee experiences. Again, a

narrative description is the usual outcome of this method. [See Mintzberg (1973) for a fascinating account of how this is done with company presidents].

5. ~~Group interview.~~ Another variation is to interview employees in small groups rather than individually. This is one way to save time, but employees may sometimes be inhibited by social pressure not to say certain things in such a public atmosphere.

6. *Work participation.* Rather than merely spending time with employees, the job analyst actually performs the job for a period of time. Clearly, this is appropriate only for a limited number of low skilled jobs.

7. *Diary.* Employees are asked to keep track of daily activities and their reactions to them. While this is a potentially useful method, it has not been used much and does depend on considerable goodwill within the organization.

8. *Technical conference.* The supervisors of employees, rather than the employees themselves, meet with and are interviewed by the job analyst. This type of information should probably be gathered, but should not be relied upon exclusively.

9. *Critical incidents.* This method (Flanagan 1954) is a variation of the interview approach in which an attempt is made to focus only on those job behaviors critical to either success or failure on the job. Each interview centers around three groups of questions: (1) What were the circumstances surrounding this specific incident? What was the context? (2) What exactly did the person do that led to effectiveness or ineffectiveness? What was the observable behavior? (3) How is this incident an example of good or bad performance? In other words, *say exactly how the behavior is linked to job performance* (Latham and Wexley 1977).

The basic approaches to job analysis: job requirements versus worker rewards. The traditional approach to job analysis gathers data pertinent to job performance, e.g., the skills, knowledge, and attitudes the person must have in order to do a competent job. Refering back to the Matching Model, it can be seen easily that this traditional focus is only part of the total picture. In addition to *performance* considerations, organizations are now starting to assess those factors that affect employee *satisfaction* and organizational *commitment*.

One type of job requirements method has been developed by the United States Department of Labor (DOL). This method is detailed in the *Handbook for Analyzing Jobs* (U.S. DOL 1972). This handbook is also directly linked to the *Dictionary of Occupational Titles* (DOT), also published by the Labor Department. The DOL approach is quite comprehensive. It includes the procedures and methods to obtain information in such areas as (1) what the worker does in relationship to data, people, and things; (2) what techniques are used; (3) what machines, tools, etc. are used; (4) what materials are worked on; and (5) what traits of the worker are required (Schneider 1976).

From the perspective of personnel selection, the most useful component of the DOL approach is the first area listed, i.e., the relationship of an employee to data, people, and things. These three "worker functions" are shown in Table 5.1. A receptionist-clerk would be coded as a 5 (Data), 6 (People), or 7 (Things). Or a dough mixer would be coded as a 5-6-2. The worker-functions approach does not explicitly incorporate different degrees of expertise within each of the functional areas. For example, the functions of a head nurse in a hospital might overlap considerably with the *functions* of a doctor, but there would be clear differences between the nures and the doctor in terms of the *level of skill* within each function (Schneider 1976).

Much of the DOL approach, while comprehensive, is cumbersome and does not yield a quantitative result; i.e., the outcome of the analysis is usually a written narrative. The Position Analysis Questionnaire (PAQ), developed at Purdue (McCormick and Tiffin 1974), is an excellent example of a quantitative method. It should be noted, however, that the PAQ is completed by a job analyst in the role of an observer–interviewer, not by the employees themselves. By using a statistical technique (factor analysis) that "sifts" through the items in search of basic categories, a total of *five basic dimensions* have been distilled from the 194 specific items on the questionnaire (McCormick and Tiffin 1974, pp. 54–55).

1. *Having decision-making/communication/social responsibilities.* This dimension reflects activities involving considerable amounts of communication and interaction with people, as well as responsibilities associated with decision-making and planning functions. A general supervisor might be engaged in such activities and have such responsibilities.

TABLE 5.1

Three types of worker functions used in the DOL job analysis

DATA	PEOPLE	THINGS
0 Synthesizing	0 Mentoring	0 Setting up
1 Coordinating	1 Negotiating	1 Precision working
2 Analyzing	2 Instructing	2 Operating—controlling
3 Compiling	3 Supervising	3 Driving—operating
4 Computing	4 Diverting	4 Manipulating
5 Copying	5 Persuading	5 Tending
6 Comparing	6 Speaking—signaling	6 Feeding—offbearing
	7 Serving	7 Handling
	8 Taking instructions— helping	

Source: U.S. DOL, 1972, p. 73, from B. Schneider, 1976, *Staffing Organizations,* Pacific Palisades, Calif.: Goodyear, p. 25.

2. *Performing skilled activities.* This dimension is characterized by activities of a skilled nature in which technical devices or tools tend to be used and in which there is an emphasis on precision, recognizing differences, and manual control. Tool and die makers are engaged in occupations that require performance of skilled activities.

3. *Being physically active/related environmental conditions.* This dimension is characterized by activities involving considerable movement of the entire body or major parts of it, along with such environments as those of factories, shops, etc.

4. *Operating vehicles/equipment.* This dimension is characterized by some aspect of the operation or use of vehicles or equipment, typically involving sensory and perceptual processes and physical functions.

5. *Processing information.* This dimension is characterized by a wide range of information-processing activities such as budget officers or editors perform. In some instances these activities are accomplished through the use of machines such as office machines.

The *worker rewards* approach is a much newer way to analyze jobs in that it represents the individual's viewpoint rather than the organization's perspective. Researchers have divided worker rewards into two types: intrinsic and extrinsic. *Intrinsic* rewards are associated with the degree of interest an individual has in the job itself. (Most leisure activities have rather high intrinsic rewards.) In contrast, *extrinsic* rewards are those out-side the task itself, given to the individual by other people.

The *total* job context is often represented by five areas that most em-ployees experience as crucial to their job satisfaction: pay, supervision, promotion opportunities, co-worker relationships, and the work itself. [See Smith, Kendall, and Hulin (1969) for the research behind these five areas.] The first four of these five are external to one's actual job duties and thus are categorized as extrinsic rewards. Obtaining satisfaction in any of these extrinsic areas depends on the actions of someone else. In contrast, intrinsic satisfaction stems directly from the work itself, with-out depending on others. Today there are standardized questionnaires available to the organization wanting to include *worker rewards* as part of a job analysis. These are relatively new developments that have emerged from research in only the last ten years.[2]

A thorough job analysis, thus, should yield information on how to best *match* newcomers in *both* ways specified by the Matching Model. That is, the *job requirements* approach provides information about how to match the abilities of people with the necessary job requirements. Simi-larly, the *worker rewards* approach indicates which people will be best matched to the organization in terms of the human needs/organizational climates fit.

Since this chapter focuses on *selection* (rather than on recruitment or organizational choice), the remainder of this discussion will concern the *job requirements* approach to job analysis. The major uses of information pertinent to the job requirements are shown in Step 2 of Fig. 5.1. The or-ganization makes two types of decisions: (1) What will be used to *estimate* the future job performance of outsiders, i.e., what *selection procedure* will be used? (2) What will be used to evaluate the performance of insiders? Step 3 in Fig. 5.1 is a rather short, logical step. To put it simply, after the decisions in Step 2 have been made, they must be implemented. The key to selection is, however, in Step 4 in which the *estimated* job performance (made at the point of entry) is related to the newcomer's *actual* job

---

[2] To measure how satisfied employees are with various aspects of an organization, the Job Descriptive Index (Smith, Kendall, and Hulin 1969) or the Minnesota Satis-faction Questionnaire (Lofquist and Dawis 1969) can be used. Both of these measure extrinsic and intrinsic aspects of the work environment. The Job Diagnostic Survey (Hackman and Oldham 1975) goes into greater detail in measuring the *intrinsic* char-acteristics of jobs.

performance. A strong relationship, or correlation, here means the selection procedure is *valid*.

What are job criteria? The word "criteria"[3] has been defined by Schneider (1976, p. 48) as

> *those behaviors and outcomes at work which competent observers can agree constitute necessary standards of excellence to be achieved in order for the individual and the organization to both accomplish their goals.*

There are three elements of this definition worthy of further comment. First, the definition includes *both* job behaviors *and* outcomes. In other words, both one's efforts and the results of those efforts are included as criteria of effective performance. Second, criteria are developed by human judgment, or as Schneider said, "competent observers." There is no easy way to devise criteria of effective job performance. Third, a two-sided perspective is taken, that of both the individual and the organization, that is perfectly consistent with the theme of this book.

What type of performance measure is taken and when are the measurements made? These two questions are basic to the development of a job performance criterion. Table 5.2 shows a wide variety of measures (some objective, some subjective) taken in three different situations (simulations, during training, and on-the-job).

The first eight measures all fall into a category that could be called "objective" since they involve numerical results of one sort or another. The last three are ratings based on human judgment. Although ratings can be numerical, too, people seem to have more faith in objective measures since human judgment appears to be less involved. The issue, then, is whether the objective methods really are superior to subjective ratings. A quick listing of the difficulties inherent in the "objective" measures should convince the reader that they, too, have problems.

The determination of rate of work is plagued by the fact that many jobs are either machine paced or so dependent on the efforts of others that it's often hard to say whether the output produced is an accurate reflection of one particular employee's efforts. The measurement of quality of

---

[3] Criteria is the plural of criterion. When only a single measure of performance is used, the term "criterion" should be used.

TABLE 5.2

Examples of job performance measures in a variety of situations

PERFORMANCE MEASURES	EVALUATIVE SITUATION		
	SIMULATED JOB PERFORMANCE	TRAINING PERFORMANCE	ACTUAL JOB PERFORMANCE
Rate of work	Amount per unit time	Time to learn	Amount per unit time
Quality of work	Ratings	Ratings	Ratings
Accidents and breakage	Accident rate	Accident rate	Accident rate
Dollars earned	Simulated earnings	Earnings	Earnings
Job knowledge		Ratings or test	Ratings or test
Job tenure		Time to learn	Length of time
Absenteeism		Number of days	Number of days
Rate of advancement	Simulated earnings	Improvement during training	Salary history—promotion history
Supervisory judgments	Ratings	Ratings	Ratings
Peer judgments	Ratings	Ratings	Ratings
Self-judgments	Ratings	Ratings	Ratings

Source: Adapted from M. L. Blum and J. C. Naylor, 1968. *Industrial Psychology: Its Theoretical and Social Foundations*, p. 196. Copyright © 1968 by Milton L. Blum and James C. Naylor. Reprinted by permission of Harper & Row, Publishers, Inc.

work is partly judgmental and partly the result of machine and materials problems beyond the control of the individual. Accidents happen for many reasons, only some of which could be called intentional poor performance. The amount of dollars earned may reflect a person's seniority more than actual job performance (Lawler 1971), or it could indicate membership in a strong union. Job tenure does not distinguish between the high performer and the person who is just barely acceptable and doesn't leave because the person has no viable alternatives. Absenteeism can be caused by genuine illness, an obvious fact too often forgotten by those wanting to use it as an indicator of low satisfaction. Finally, promotions may be based on seniority as much as on job performance.

Rating of employees by superiors has been the traditional way most managers are appraised. Peer ratings have been used primarily in the military in contrast to most businesses that have used them for research purposes only (Lewin and Zwany 1977). Self-ratings are increasingly being used by organizations that encourage personal career planning. In such cases, self-ratings are *not* part of one's performance assessment. Rather, they are usually kept secret by personnel staff members responsible for career counseling, so that one's own boss does not have access to them (Hall 1976).

There are several methods to rate employees, as shown in Fig. 5.2. Types a, b, and c are purely numerical, having no written definitions for the scale points. The graphic scales show various ways to help the rater understand what each of the numbered scale points means.

Three major problems beset such scales: (1) halo effect, (2) leniency, or harshness, and (3) central tendency. The halo effect refers to the rating error made when the evaluator fails to discriminate among various aspects of the person being rated, e.g., effort, promotability; ratings are based on a single general impression, either good or bad. Leniency (or harshness) refers to a rater who tends to rate all employees at one or the other extreme ends of the scale. Central tendency refers to the lumping of all ratees in the middle of the scale, a type of "fence-straddling" by the rater, who may be hesitant to make extremely high or low ratings.

Graphic rating scales are used by *at least* 80 percent of business organizations. There are guidelines that should be followed to achieve maximum effectiveness from such scales: (1) the language should be kept simple, (2) universal terms such as "always" or "never" should be avoided,

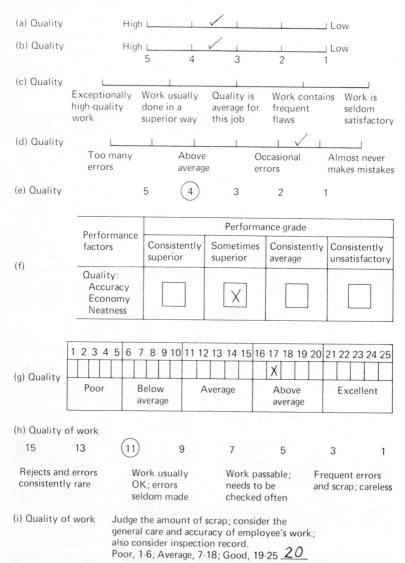

Fig. 5.2 *Examples of numerical and graphic rating scales. (From R. M. Guion, 1965,* Personnel Testing, *p. 98. Reprinted by permission of the McGraw-Hill Book Publishing Company.)*

(3) between 5-9 scale points should be used, (4) no more than five factors should be rated, and (5) the frame of reference should be constant; i.e., it should not shift back and forth between "on the job" or "in general."

ASSESSMENT OF JOB CANDIDATES

The first section of this chapter focused more on the *job* than on the *person*. Here the focus is on the job candidates themselves who seek entry into a new organization. Four topics are covered:

1. Testing, which includes testing for aptitudes, achievement, and motivation

2. The meaning of test reliability and validity

3. Interviewing of candidates

4. The assessment center method for selection.

The last topic will receive extensive coverage, since it is an important new development.

Selection Testing

Testing for organizational selection is done for a variety of purposes. First, it is helpful to know what the individual is *presently able to do,* based on the individual's education, training, and work experiences. Such tests are called "achievement" tests. Achievement tests are often helpful in analyzing how easy it will be for persons to enter a particular job and be successful at it. Generally speaking, however, achievement tests do *not* directly indicate the *potential* of the person for future growth or for doing other jobs, nor do they indicate how *motivated* that person will be in a particular situation. To assess these latter two concerns, organizations have used *aptitude* tests to estimate potential. They have used a variety of *personality, interest, and temperament* tests to indicate how "motivated" an individual will be.

Of these three types of selection tests, *aptitude* tests are usually the best predictors of both success in training and on-the-job performance (Ghiselli 1966). *Motivation* tests are poor predictors of job performance, but can be used to predict (1) what occupations people are likely to enter (2) how satisfied people will be in an occupation, (3) what organizations will be chosen, and (4) the length of one's tenure in a particular organization (Schneider 1976). Finally, achievement tests are usually considered to be the end-result of activities (like the bar exam for lawyers) rather than predictors of future job performance. Thus they have not been used as often for employee selection as have aptitude tests. Recently, there has been governmental and legal pressure to hire educationally disadvantaged persons based on their aptitudes, not their current achievement. This is in recognition of the fact that past deficits in educational or job opportunities will have a greater impact on current achievement levels than future potential (Schneider 1976).

Achievement tests. An achievement test is similar to an aptitude test in the sense that it tests "maximum" performance. It differs from "typical performance" tests (such as personality, interest, or motivation tests). In general, an achievement test is designed to assess the degree to which someone has already acquired either a body of knowledge or certain skills.

There are three types of achievement tests: (1) recognition, (2) simulated conditions, and (3) work-sample tests (Ryans and Frederiksen 1971). Recognition tests are those in which an evaluator is shown the *outcome* of a person's effort, e.g., a poem, a song, or a radio that the person has repaired. Schneider (1976) has pointed out that such tests are able only to tap the *end result* of one's efforts and cannot evaluate the correctness of the *procedures* used. Tests of simulated conditions are commonly used in military training, where such simulations were popularized during Office of Strategic Services (OSS) training in World War II. The best modern-day example is the use of the *in-basket technique* (Frederickson, Saunders, and Wand 1957) that tries to simulate a wide variety of business activities a manager might have to cope with, e.g., routine letters and crisis situations. Finally, in a work-sample test one performs the actual, not the simulated, task. (See Table 3.5 for a list.)

Motivation tests. A wide variety of tests fall into the general category called "motivation" testing. These tests all try to measure the *typical* behavior (or attitudes) of an individual. There are three categories of "motivation" tests (Guion 1965): (1) interest tests, (2) personality tests, and (3) preferences for certain types of jobs.

Interest tests are probably familiar to most readers because they are usually given in high schools for counseling purposes. Interest tests predict the *occupations* individuals enter, rather than specific organizations. Interest tests predict how *satisfied* people will be in certain occupations, rather than how well they will *perform* in an occupation.

Personality tests fall into three categories. The first category is called *rative,* which means that the test has items calling for an evaluative judgment by the test taker—a rating of some sort. Multiple-choice tests are the second type. Both rative and multiple-choice tests call for responses that are more structured than are the responses called for by projective tests. They also call for an explicit description of oneself. In contrast to these, *projective* tests usually try to have people give *unrestricted* responses to an open-ended or ambiguous question. The assumption is that oneself is "projected" into the answers given.

The third category of motivation tests concerns the preferences of employees for particular types of jobs. The attempt to measure preferences for one's ideal job is a rather direct, straightforward way to obtain the data necessary to match human needs to the reward climates of an organization. The other types of motivation tests are very *indirect.* They assume that there is a link either between occupational interests or personality on the one hand and one's preferences for a job on the other. The Survey of Work Values (Wollack, Goodale, Wijting, and Smith 1971) is designed to measure an individual's "orientation to work" *in general,* rather than the individual's orientation to a *specific* job. The Job Diagnostic Survey (JDS) is, however, aimed at one's *preferences for a specific job* (Hackman and Oldham 1974a and 1974b, 1975). Thus the JDS is probably the most useful instrument for diagnosing *both* job conditions (see the earlier "worker rewards" discussion) *and* personal preferences necessary to match human needs to the various internal climates of the organization. Table 5.3 shows sample items from the JDS designed to measure the preferences (human needs) of people for certain types of jobs.

In theory, motivation tests could be used by organizations to match the needs of newcomers to organizational climates in much the same way as they match results of various selection tests with job requirements. (This is a highly desirable objective. In Chapters 2 and 3 the realisitc recruitment method was described as one way to accomplish this objective by having newcomers *self*-select themselves into the organization.) From the organizational viewpoint of personnel selection, is it also possible that

TABLE 5.3

Sample items from the Job Diagnostic Survey

Listed below are a number of characteristics that could be present on any job. People differ about how much they would like to have each one present in their own jobs. We are interested in learning *how much you personally would like* to have each one present in your job.

Using the scale below, please indicate the *degree* to which you *would like* to have each characteristic present in your job.

Note: The numbers on this scale are different from those used in previous scales.

4	5	6	7	8	9	10
Would mildly like having this			Would strongly like having this			Would very strongly like having this

_____ 1. High respect and fair treatment from my supervisor

_____ 2. Stimulating and challenging work

_____ 3. Chances to exercise independent thought and action in my job

_____ 4. Great job security

_____ 5. Very friendly co-workers

_____ 6. Opportunities to learn new things from my work

_____ 7. High salary and good fringe benefits

_____ 8. Opportunities to be creative and imaginative in my work

_____ 9. Quick promotions

_____10. Opportunities for personal growth and development in my job

_____11. A sense of worthwhile accomplishment in my work

Source: J. R. Hackman and G. R. Oldham, 1974a, *The Job Diagnostic Survey: An Instrument for the Diagnosis of Jobs and the Evaluation of Job Redesign Projects.* New Haven: Yale School of Organization and Management, Technical Report 4, May.

organizations can do a better job of matching by using motivation tests. Despite the desirability of this, the prospects seem quite dim for reasons that are discussed below. (See Guion 1965 or Schneider 1976 for further discussion of the problems involved in using motivation tests.)

The major problem involved in using motivation tests of "typical" performance is that the answers are easy to fake. Faking answers becomes serious the more obvious the purpose of the test is to the person taking it. Guion (1965) has gone so far as to suggest that test developers take another long, hard look at such *indirect* measures of interest as reading preferences, collections, hobbies, and preferences for leisure activities. A second problem involved in using motivation testing is that most of the personality tests were *not* constructed to be used in employment situations and may be so clinically oriented as to have no obvious relationship to job situations. Because this is true there is the additional problem that job candidates may see the test as an invasion of privacy.

We have now reviewed the basic categories of tests. The next issue to explore is how accurate the tests are as selection tools. In order to evaluate selection tests properly, the reader must understand the two basic concepts of reliability and validity, since these are the two ways to evaluate tests.

Reliability. The concept of reliability refers to the *consistency* of a particular measurement procedure. There are three ways to assess the degree of consistency of selection tests: (1) test-retest, (2) internal comparison of items, e.g., odd versus even numbered items, and (3) using equivalent forms of the test (Dunnette 1966).

To illustrate each of these three types of determining reliability, let's take an example of a company with an aptitude test of 100 items intended to measure problem-solving ability and judgment for managerial decision making. To assess consistency of the test over time, the test–retest method could be used. This method requires those who took the test at one time to take it again at a later time. Generally speaking, the longer the interval between tests, the lower the test-retest reliability. More factors can intervene in a long interval than can in a short interval.

Another way to measure consistency is to take the 100 items, divide them into two groups, and then evaluate the relationship between scores on the two groups of items, usually by computing a correlation coefficient. The most common way to divide test items is by using an odd-even split. This would mean computing two test scores for each person (odd and even) and then correlating these scores for as many persons as took the test.[4] The third way to estimate test reliability is to construct two tests, both equivalent to one another. When this is done, the usual procedure is to administer one test and then the other as a retest some time later, say a month. It should be obvious that this method does require quite a bit of extra work.

Thus test reliability refers to both stability over time as well as to consistency at a particular point in time. Since test reliability does have both

---

[4] The correlation obtained should then be "corrected" by the Spearman–Brown formula. See any basic text on testing, e.g., Guion (1965).

these meanings, the particular method used to estimate test reliability must be identified.

Reliability is a statement about the test's relationship *with itself,* rather than with something else. Regardless of whether one refers to reliability in the stability of consistency sense, it is still a statement about the *test itself* and *not* the relationship of the test to other types of job behavior, e.g., job performance. The *validity* of a test refers to its correlation with various aspects of job behavior, e.g., performance, absenteeism, turnover, accidents, and so forth.

The relationships between reliability and validity may not be clear to those first exposed to these concepts. The critical thing to remember is that reliability is a necessary, but not a sufficient, cause of test validity. Figure 5.3 shows the possible relationships between reliability and validity.

		Is the selection procedure reliable?	
		Yes	No
Is the selection procedure valid?	Yes	Possible, and desirable	Not possible
	No	Possible, and potentially misleading	Possible, but not desirable

Fig 5.3 *Relationships between reliability and validity.*

Validity. Organizations have used two basic methods to assess the validity of a selection procedure: (1) criterion-related validity, and (2) content validity. The criterion-related method of determining selection procedure validity[5] is an assessment of the type of relationship between the specific measure used for job performance and that used to select newcomers. In content validity, expert opinion is used to estimate the *relevance* of a particular selection procedure. The crucial difference is that no actual job performance data are collected when content validity is used.

---

[5] "Procedure" is a more inclusive term than "test" because a test may be one part of the procedure. Interviews and simulated job experiences might also be used, and their validity assessed.

There are two types of criterion-related validity; the difference between them depends on the timing of data collection. *Concurrent* validity means that both predictor (e.g., score on a selection test) *and* criterion measures are obtained at the same time. A common example is the organization that is trying to develop a new predictor of job success. In this case the personnel department might obtain a group of employees already on the job and administer the proposed selection technique. At the same time they could obtain job performance evaluations from the supervisors of those employees. The relationship between these two sets of data, expressed as a correlation coefficient, is concurrent validity.

Although the concurrent validity approach seems simple enough, it is flawed because those persons included in the study may not be a representative sample of the kinds of people who are job candidates. Job applicants are usually much more diverse than any group of employees already inside the organization.

Predictive validity is the second type of criterion-related validity. The predictor data (e.g., selection test scores) are gathered *prior* to entry, and the criterion data (job performance) are gathered *after* entry, e.g., at the completion of training or after several months on the job.

The major problem involved in conducting a thorough predictive validity study is that organizations may be tempted to use the proposed selection test as part of the hiring decision. To give the selection procedure being studied a fair evaluation, it is important that the data collected at entry *not* be used in selection decisions. To use these data is undesirable because their use presumes the procedure to be valid when the determination of the validity of the procedure is the purpose of the study in the first place. A second reason is that only those with "high" scores would be hired. Thus the organization cannot evaluate how those people with "low" scores would have done if they had been hired.

Finally, *content validity* is an assessment (expert judgment) of how relevant a test is for the prediction of success on a job. For example, holding an M.D. degree is considered to be a prerequisite for practicing medicine. This is a judgment that has not been established by criterion-related validity. Arvey's (1979) recent book on selection concludes that content validity is going to be an increasingly popular (*and legal*) method to justify selection procedures.

Validity of tests for prediction of success. One comprehensive review of testing covered 1919 to mid-1964 (Ghiselli 1966) and was updated through 1972 (Ghiselli 1973). This review related various selection test scores to two criteria: (1) success in training, and (2) on-the-job performance. The details of these reviews are not discussed here. Only the overall trends will be reviewed because they are what has caught the attention of others (e.g., Ash and Kroeker 1975). First, based on both the original review and its update, it is easier to predict success in training than to predict success on the job. The average correlation, over all studies reviewed, between selection tests and training was .30 in the original review and .39 in the update. In contrast, the average correlation between tests and job performance was .19 in the original and .22 in the update. Second, Ghiselli noted that an overall average *understates the actual state of the art because *all* tests are included, not just the best ones.* By restricting the review to *best tests* for predicting training or performance, the average validities increased. In the original study the average correlation for *best* tests was .47 with training and .33 for performance. In the update these were .45 with training and .35 for performance.

The interpretation of correlations used to express test validity is a particularly tricky business. Legally speaking, it is necessary that test validity be "statistically significant," i.e., that the probability of error is less than 5 percent. If Ghiselli is correct in stating that the average validity for best tests is .35, *is this high or low?*

The first point in trying to interpret a correlation is that one always looks at the specific situation. For example, a validity of .35 may be statistically significant in one situation, but not in another. This can happen because the number of people taking the test influences statistical significance. This ought to make good sense because it is logical to have more confidence in a validity of .35 when it is based on a group of 100 instead of 30. The more people studied, the greater the confidence that can be placed in the result. Statistical tables take the number of people studied into consideration. For example, to reach the customary level of statistical significance (5 percent chance of error) it takes a correlation of .35 for a sample of 30, .27 for 50, .20 for 100, .14 for 100, and only .09 for a group of 500. Thus it's nearly impossible to make any overall statement about whether an average test validity is high or low.

The Interview

The interview has traditionally been used for a number of purposes, e.g., to recruit newcomers (see Chapter 4), to select them, to place them on appropriate jobs, to counsel employees, to diagnose attitude problems among personnel, and to see how people respond to stressful situations. This discussion of the interview is limited to the selection process. Within personnel selection itself, however, it is possible (and important) to distinguish among several functions of the interview.

The effects of an interview on organization entry fall into two basic categories. The interview can affect the match between employee abilities and job requirements or it can influence the match between human needs and organizational climates. Considering the former match, interviews have been used to assess both the aptitudes of job candidates, as well as past achievements. Evidence collected over the last thirty years (reviewed by Mayfield 1964; Osburn and Constantin 1977; Schmitt 1976, Ulrich and Trumbo 1965; Wagner 1949; Wright 1969) clearly indicates that interviews are a *very poor* way to assess *aptitudes*. In fact, Schneider (1976, p. 194) has gone so far as to state:

> The choice of whether or not to use the verbal (interview) or paper-and-pencil (questionnaire) method for collecting potentially valid background information is really the only legitimate decision one can make regarding the usefulness of the preemployment interview.

Schneider is saying that interviews (or application forms) are pretty good at uncovering background information about job candidates that might be relevant for job performance, i.e., assessment of *achievements* rather than *aptitudes*.

Interviews are, however, potentially useful methods to match employee *needs* with the organizational climates. This matching can happen in two ways. First, employee needs can be assessed by obtaining factual information about past activities. How people spend their leisure time may give the interviewer insight into whether an individual will be satisfied with a job of high, medium, or low stress. The degree to which a person prefers cooperative activities (team sports, or doubles in tennis) may indicate needs for certain types of jobs in contrast with those who prefer situations in which they alone have responsibility (golf, or singles in tennis). The second "needs-climates matching function" is that interviews are two-way conversations and *may* provide information to job candidates helpful in making *their own* organizational choices. This *potential* use of the interview is usually not realized because of traditional recruitment philosophies that increase the conflicts between individual and organization during entry (see Fig. 2.1).

In Chapter 4 two research findings about the interview were discussed because they were relevant to helping individuals make their own organizational choices. The findings were that (1) negative information carries greater weight than positive information, and (2) the early part of the interview is the most crucial part. In this section several other conclusions are covered that show why interviews are poor ways to assess the aptitudes of job candidates.

First, some interviewers tend to develop personal stereotypes about the ideal job candidate. Typically, interviewers can agree on the relevant factors for a desirable job candidate, but are usually unable to agree whether or not to hire a particular person. One solution to this problem is to provide more information to interviewers, particularly information that is stated in terms of actual behavior.

Second, the judgments of interviewers may be affected by the degree of similarity between interviewer and job candidate. Although many believe that both women and blacks will get low evaluations from white, male interviewers, the most up-to-date reviews of the research indicate these beliefs are not substantiated (Arvey 1979; Osburn and Constantin 1977). A person's job qualifications are much more important in an interviewer's evaluation than either the race or sex of the candidate, although race and sex do have an influence on interviewer assessments.

A third characteristic of interviews is called the "contrast effect." Contrast effect refers to the tendency of interviewers to change their evaluations from one candidate to the next based on the contrast between them. This tendency may be a serious source of unreliability. However, these changes might also represent learning and growth on the part of the interviewer (Osburn and Constantin 1977). Inexperienced interviewers, or those interviewing candidates for a job that is unfamiliar to the interviewers, may be expected to show the contrast effect because they are still learning about the job. However, if contrast effects are found among the most experienced of interviewers, they represent a source of unreliability.

The Assessment Center Method

The *combination* of many *different techniques* to assess job candidates in a short, but intensive experience has been called the *assessment center*. This comprehensive approach, which emphasizes the use of simulations, has historical roots that go back to World War II in the selection (and training) of intelligence officers for the Office of Strategic Services (OSS 1948). The pioneering study of this in business is the Management Progress Study done at AT&T. This study is unique and particularly noteworthy because the data gathered during the assessment process were *not* used in hiring decisions. Rather, AT&T continued to use existing methods and standards while the new, assessment center approach was being tested. Today a number of other organizations, e.g., IBM, GE, Ford, GM, Sears, American Airlines, Bendix, GTE, Merrill Lynch, SOHIO, have adopted this approach to personnel selection, particularly for management and supervisory positions. This approach is also used by government agencies, e.g., HUD, HEW, the FBI, Civil Service Commission, the Social Security Administration, the Air Force, and the Equal Employment Opportunity Commission.

Discussion of the assessment center method will be rather lengthy because it is a significant innovation in organizational selection. Several topics will be covered: (1) the different objectives an assessment center can fulfill, (2) the types of job dimensions it can assess, (3) the types of exercises that compose an assessment center, (4) how assessors are selected and trained, (5) how job candidates are selected for assessment, (6) the logic, or theory underlying why assessment centers accurately predict later success on the job, and (7) illustrative results from AT&T's original study.

Assessment center objectives. Three basic objectives can be met by an assessment center: (1) personnel selection, (2) individual development, and (3) appraisal of management potential (Jeswald 1977). The specific design of a center depends, then, on the particular objective that is of importance. Because these three objectives are different from each other, it is nearly impossible to meet all three using the same design and procedures. Table 5.4 shows how the design of an assessment center changes according to the type of objective that it is to meet.

Personnel selection is the most common objective of assessment centers today. In some cases the job candidates come from outside the

TABLE 5.4

Differences in assessment center design according to assessment objective

ASPECTS OF THE CENTER DESIGN	OBJECTIVE OF ASSESSMENT		
	SELECTION	DEVELOPMENT	APPRAISAL OF POTENTIAL
Basis for selecting target job	Immediate need for qualified personnel	Immediate need to upgrade skills or broaden experiences of present managers or those identified as possessing "potential"	Long-term need to identify and develop a pool of qualified management personnel
Eligibility for participation	Those qualified by experience or education for a specific position	Those identified as having skills deficiencies or narrow experience	Those performing well on supervisory or staff specialist jobs
Nature of the skills assessed	Specific: limited to skills critical for performance of the target job	May be specific or general	Generalizable to a family of management jobs
Time required for assessment	Minimum necessary to simulate critical tasks and maintain reliability of measurement	Minimum necessary to simulate critical tasks, provide immediate feedback and/or counseling	Minimum necessary to simulate critical tasks, provide immediate feedback and/or counseling
Difficulty level of assessment exercises	No more difficult than the most difficult tasks required in the target job	Various levels of difficulty, so that participants with different degrees of competence can be challenged	Various levels of difficulty, so that participants with different degrees of competence can be identified
Type of decision reached	Select or reject for the target job	Need for other developmental experiences	Need for developmental experiences, eligibility for future promotions

Extent of feedback given	Limited	Detailed: may include peer and self-evaluations	Detailed: may include peer evaluations; emphasizes goal setting with the supervisor, career planning, and self-development
Reports generated	Brief: retained by the personnel office	Detailed: retained by the participant and training specialists	Detailed: retained by the participant and the personnel office
Follow-up research required	1. Validation, as required by government regulations 2. Continuous monitoring of reliability 3. Development of new exercises and alternate forms	None: measurement of behavior change is highly desirable	1. Validation, as required by government regulations 2. Continuous monitoring of reliability 3. Development of new exercises and alternative forms 4. Measurement of behavior change

Source: T. A. Jeswald, 1977. Issues in establishing an assessment center. In J. L. Moses and W. C. Byham (eds.), *Applying the Assessment Center Method*, pp. 50–51. Reprinted by permission of Pergamon Press.

organization, and in others from inside the organization at lower level jobs. Using the assessment center method for appraisal of management potential is slightly different since the job-to-be-filled is *not* the one a successful candidate immediately enters. In this case the organization is trying to identify who might move up and into higher level jobs after sufficient job experience (as in the AT&T Management Progress Study predicting who would be promoted to the third-level of management). The least common, but growing, use of assessment centers is to provide feedback to individuals on their strengths and weaknesses for individual development. The key to this last objective is to give maximum *feedback* to the participant. In some cases videotape equipment is used to provide an accurate account of what went on during each exercise, so the participant can view his or her own behavior and also have the benefit of observations from the assessment staff.

Defining assessment dimensions. As in the case with more traditional se-lection procedures, *job analysis* (see Fig. 5.1) is the crucial starting point. There simply is *no single, comprehensive list of job dimensions for man-agement jobs*. There are differences that stem from both the *functional area* and from the *level* in the organization. In this sense, then, a job analy-sis must be done for *each* job type of concern in an assessment center.

After a complete job analysis, the choice of what behavioral dimen-sions to include in the assessment center is made by considering three criteria. First of all the general dimensions must be defined clearly. For example "communication skills" could be defined as the abilities to

- pick out important information
- listen alertly
- give feedback to others
- listen for a purpose
- recognize barriers to good listening and overcome them
- understand another's point of view
- keep language simple and to the point
- use sketches or diagrams in a report or talk
- make helpful summations

The second consideration in selecting basic dimensions is the cost of doing so. In some cases it may be cheaper to appraise certain technical skills outside the assessment center. For example, passing the Certified Public Accounting exam could be a substitute for the *technical* requirements of a financial officer, whereas the assessment center would evaluate *managerial* skills.

The third consideration in selecting dimensions for the center is how well they will fit the existing performance appraisal system used by an organization. This is a problem today because assessment centers are new relative to performance appraisal systems (Jeswald 1977).

The actual number of behavioral dimensions included varies from job to job and organization to organization within a range of 10–25 (Howard 1974). The AT&T Management Progress Study used 25, e.g., organizing and planning, oral and written communication skills, flexibility, forcefulness, leadership, energy, resistance to stress, inner work standards, originality, and human relations competence.

Exercises Used to Assess Candidates

A rather wide variety of exercises has been devised to simulate conditions encountered on a job (Crooks 1977). One particular exercise will typically allow assessors to observe some, but not all, of the dimensions composing the job. The job candidate in completing all the exercises provides the assessor several different opportunities to observe a particular dimension. For example, the in-basket exercise (see below) enables the assessor to observe a person's judgment, tolerance of stress, organizing ability and initiative, but it does *not* provide the assessor the opportunity to observe oral communication, listening skills, or flexibility.

The *in-basket exercise* is probably the most commonly used of all those discussed here. The job candidate is provided with background material, references, and a "package" of problems to be handled. The problems have their own priorities, relationships to each other, and time deadlines. The candidate is given a specified time period and asked to assume the role of the manager. In-basket exercises have been developed for all levels of management, from the first level to senior executive levels.

Several *management games* are also used. For example, AT&T first used a team exercise on the manufacturing of a prototype product using

Tinkertoys. This was followed by a stock market game and others. Although the use of Tinkertoys may seem absurd, it increases the possibility of injecting a great deal of realism into such a game. For example, many of the same elements and job pressures can be part of the simulation: competition among teams, problems of continuous supply of materials, cost of maintaining an inventory, costs of poor quality production, time deadlines, etc.

Leaderless group discussions are also used. These can have either non-assigned or assigned roles for the participants to play. With nonassigned roles each person is given several short cases concerning various management problems. Each acts as a consultant, giving whatever ideas he or she comes up with, and sometimes makes a written summary. An example of assigned roles is a city-council simulation used by American Airlines (Rice 1978, p. 100):

> That evening, the men split into groups of five for an exercise in which they played the role of city councillors responsible for either the police, fire, health, highway, or sanitation departments. The city had just received a $1 million federal grant, and each councillor had to make an oral presentation in which he tried to get as much as possible for his own department's needs. He based his argument on a two-page briefing sheet. Since all the needs amounted to several million dollars, the council had to reach a compromise—within a one-hour deadline—totaling exactly $1 million.

Oral presentation exercises. Because many managers are often asked to make presentations before a group or an audience, several exercises have been designed to simulate this. The exact nature of the presentation varies, e.g., financial analysis, new product development, sales strategy, new programs in human resources, etc. Typically, the job candidate receives a package of unorganized data. After a period of time—as in a "homework assignment"—the candidate prepares the talk. Oftentimes those in the group (other job candidates) are encouraged to ask questions, thereby adding realism to the exercise.

Role-playing simulations. A wide variety of role-playing exercises to simulate "one-on-one" encounters has been devised. For example, there is a call from an irate customer that the candidate must handle, a counseling interview with a troubled subordinate, a hiring interview, a performance appraisal interview, etc. Virtually any type of typical human interaction can be simulated through role playing.

Writing exercises. Job candidates may be asked to take "raw" information and use it to complete various types of forms, questionnaires, etc. Sometimes they are asked to write an essay on a particular topic.

Paper-and-pencil tests. These are the "classic" psychological tests that try to measure the aptitudes, motivation, or achievements of a job candidate. Increasingly, however, these are being used for research purposes only rather than being used to make the final judgment on hiring. Because the other components of the assessment center *appear* to be much more *job related,* they are more likely to avoid legal challenges. Most psychological tests, however, usually do not look job related and are, therefore, open to immediate suspicion by job candidates.

Selection and training of assessors. In the early days of the assessment center method, it was thought that only trained industrial psychologists with Ph.D.s could be assessors, as was the case in the original AT&T Management Progress Study. Today, however, managers from the organizations themselves (and sometimes professional psychologists) are used as assessors (Byham 1977). This raises the two issues of how such managers are selected and how they are trained for this important responsibility. Assessors are usually two levels above the present level of job candidates, and thus one level above that for which the candidates are being considered. In hiring or promoting executives, such as vice presidents, outside consultants are often used because so few senior executives are available.

Since the assessment center consumes a great deal of time, most organizations rotate managers into and out of the role of assessor. The most typical procedure is to train several managers at various levels to act as assessors. However, AT&T often puts a manager into a six-month stint as an assessor. Unlike AT&T, those organizations that rotate managers use them once or twice a year and usually not more than four times.

There are some advantages in training a relatively large pool of assessors within the organization. First, involving people in this method is an excellent way to build their commitment to it. This reduces fear of and resistance to the assessment center. Second, to be trained as an assessor increases the diagnostic skills of a manager, so that better performance reviews can be conducted. One problem caused by having managers participate widely as assessors is that some assessors may become assessees at some future time. Obviously, this can be a problem, but it is possible to change the exercises so that there will not be any unfair advantage. Despite this, however, those who have not been trained as assessors may still believe they are at a disadvantage to those who have been trained.

A relatively large number of assessors is needed because the ratio of assessors to assessees is either one to one or one to two. It is too difficult for most assessors to observe *and document* (in writing) the behavior of more than two job candidates.

Another issue in selection of assessors is whether they should be line or staff managers. The advantage of using line managers is their greater familiarity with the job. Often a company, to keep the image of the center as a line operation, will try to have not more than about half of the assessors from staff sources. Finally, most companies try to prevent job candidates from being assessed by any of their prior acquaintances. This is usually easy to accomplish in larger organizations.

Assessor *training* is also quite a complex process. It involves at least *six* aspects (Byham 1977): (1) understanding the basic dimensions for the job, (2) being able to observe another person's behavior during the exercises, (3) categorizing the observed behavior into the appropriate basic dimensions, (4) rating each dimension in terms of how much it was shown during the exercise, (5) being able to process information from a variety of exercises so that a consensus among assessors can be reached on each dimension, and (6) reaching an overall judgment about a job candidate's hirability, promotability, or training needs.

Byham (1977) has argued that training in understanding the *basic dimensions* used for the assessment is crucial. If assessors do not understand, *and agree on,* the definitions of them, they will spend too much time arguing about the dimensions rather than observing the behavior. Byham suggests five key elements in this aspect of assessor training: (1) use dimensions based on a thorough job analysis that the assessors understand (preferably one in which they took part); (2) keep the number of dimensions small; (3) have short, clear definitions for each one; (4) give clear behavioral examples of what might be observed in each exercise; and

(5) have practice sessions in which assessors categorize behavioral observations into the basic dimensions.

Training in the *observation of behavior* involves getting assessors to recognize the distinction between *specific behaviors* and *general* statements or *evaluations* of a person's behavior. For example, it is *not* correct for an assessor to say, "the candidate seemed confident." It *is* correct to say, "The candidate spoke without the use of notes." The former is a *conclusion* reached by the observer, whereas the latter is an example of a specific, observable piece of behavior. One way this training is done is to have assessors read through a series of one-sentence statements and classify them as either good examples of *behavior* or as poor examples (because they were too vague or reached a conclusion).

Training in the classifying of behavior into basic dimensions follows a similar course. A number of statements are presented to assessors and they are to judge which dimension the statement best represents. As with the preceding example, there are right answers and wrong answers, so the assessor trainees get immediate feedback on their performance at this task. Group discussions and the help of experienced assessors facilitate the learning of this skill.

After the assessors have categorized behavioral observations into the correct dimensions, they *rate each dimension in terms of how much observable behavior is available*. This is important because the usual procedure is for assessors to discuss each candidate on a dimension-by-dimension basis. If there is agreement that little evidence is available for a particular dimension, this must be taken into account prior to a final, overall rating.

Finally, assessors must be trained in processing complex information both *within* each dimension and *across* dimensions to reach an *overall rating*. They need training in how to reach a *group consensus* for each job candidate. According to Byham (1977), this is the *least* emphasized component of assessor training. The reason seems to be that experienced managers have already developed the capacity to process information and to work effectively in groups. Apparently the skills necessary to do the earlier steps in the assessment process are *not* encountered in the typical managerial job. Therefore, special training is needed if one is to become a competent assessor.

Figure 5.4 shows how assessment center information is processed by the typical organization. Depending on the basic objective of the center (as discussed earlier), the flow could be "heavier" on the feedback side (left side). In cases in which the center is used for selection, more information would flow on the right-hand side of the diagram.

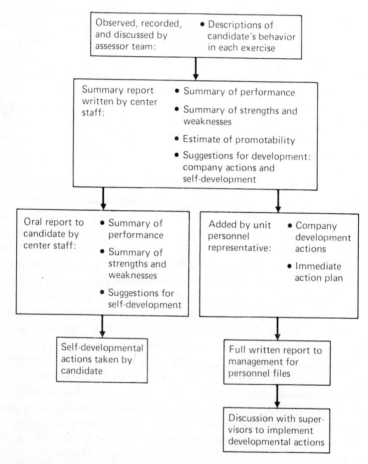

Fig. 5.4 *Flow of assessment information. From T. A. Jeswald, 1977, Issues in establishing an assessment center. In J. L. Moses and W. C. Byham (eds.),* Applying the Assessment Center Method, *p. 65. Reprinted by permission of Pergamon Press.)*

Selection of job candidates for assessment. When outsiders are being assessed for hiring purposes, the typical practice is to assess all of them for the particular job. Selection of assessees is more complicated when insiders are assessed for promotion or for identification of upper management potential.

Typically, employees are nominated for the assessment center by their immediate supervisors, although self-nomination is often used by some organizations.

What happens if a person does not do well in the center? Most companies, e.g., AT&T, discourage a second chance at assessment. They have found the method to provide *reliable* (i.e., repeatable or stable) results. Requests for a second assessment are accepted if the person can substantiate the claim that he or she has had significant new experiences and has made significant progress in terms of personal development.

The theory and logical basis for assessment centers. A major logical appeal of the method is that *behavior* is predicted from *behavior* (Holmes 1977; Rice 1978). Note that various psychological tests are *not* the same as the work-oriented exercises used in assessment centers. For example, "motivation tests" ask the person what he or she *would* do, not what the person actually does. To assess the latter, the company has to provide an opportunity for the person to demonstrate interpersonal competence, etc., as in assessment center exercises.

A second element in the success of assessment centers is the fact that behavior is observed by several persons, not just one. This increases the degree of confidence in the data obtained. When the final judgment is made, it is made by *group consensus* that has been shown to increase the accuracy of such judgments (Hoffman 1965; Hackman and Morris 1975).

When assessment centers are used to make promotional decisions, an issue is whether or not this method is superior to the annual rating of one's performance done by a superior. The assessment center would appear to have several advantages over such ratings:

- *The assessors have no direct working relationship, nor are they acquainted in any way with the assessees. Therefore, assessors tend to be more objective.*

- *Assessors are trained to be* observers *and* recorders *of behavior. They* do not evaluate the behavior until after the exercises are completed. This avoids the pitfall of the (often incorrect) first impression.

- The exercises in the center are standardized so that all job candidates have an equal opportunity to demonstrate their abilities.

- The exercises can be used to simulate a wide range of job types and levels. Thus it is easier to assess people for a promotion than to make a recommendation based only on how well they do their present job.

- The typical manager is deficient in the ability to accurately observe behavior, code it, and evaluate it. A typical problem for traditional performance appraisal is that a subordinate who has "been known for two years" may actually be known only for a rather limited range of behavior that gets repeated daily.

AN EXAMPLE OF A SUCCESSFUL ASSESSMENT CENTER: THE AT&T MANAGEMENT PROGRESS STUDY

This is *the* study (Bray, Campbell, and Grant 1974) that paved the way for the current popularity of assessment centers. It began in 1956 and is still continuing today! This makes it the longest running study of managerial behavior in existence. The basic objective of this study was the identification of managerial talent. The assessment center procedure used in this study was *not* used to hire newcomers. Rather, newcomers were hired according to existing AT&T procedures. All who were hired, however, were assessed and the results kept secret by personnel research so as not to bias the results by creating either the "crown prince" or "kiss of death" effects—both of which are examples of the *self-fulfilling prophecy*.

A total of 274 managers were hired between 1956 and 1960, but the size of this group had shrunk to 123 at the eight-year follow-up and to 110 at the sixteen-year follow-up. The job candidates went through three and a half days of assessment exercises; the assessors in this case were professional industrial psychologists hired by AT&T. The remaining one and a half days of the week were devoted to the assessor meetings about each candidate; about one and a half hours were devoted to each of 12 candidates who were assessed each week.

The job candidates played a two-hour business game concerned with the buying of parts, assembly of materials, and selling of the finished product—using Tinkertoys. There was a group discussion problem lasting one hour during which each participant was to "champion" one of his or her own employees for a promotion. However, because the group could select only one and had to reach a consensus, the in-basket was used. An assessee worked on it for three hours and was then interviewed by an assessor about the strategy used to organize the work.

Besides participating in these simulations of managerial work, each candidate was interviewed for about two hours, completed a 120-item test of current affairs, and did several *projective* tests. (A projective test presents a person with an ambiguous picture, and the person is instructed to write a story about it. The idea is that the person "projects" his or her own feelings into the story. It is a motivation type of test.) Finally, an IQ test was also administered.

At the end of the three and a half days the assessors discussed all the data for each person and came to a group consensus about the management potential of each job candidate. The assessors were concerned with one basic prediction. Would this job candidate be promoted to the third level of management (i.e., "middle management") within ten years? It was a simple "yes–no" prediction, with no room for vascillation.

How accurate were these predictions? Figures 5.5, 5.6, and 5.7 show the results. Figure 5.5 shows the accuracy of these predictions made at an eight-year follow-up. From this figure it can be seen that $39/61 = 64$ percent of those predicted to make third level within ten years had actually done so during the eight-year period. In contrast, only $20/62 = 32$ percent made middle management from among those predicted *not* to make it. The difference between 64 and 32 percent is considered to be quite an impressive difference, particularly when it is remembered that the predictions were made *eight years* earlier after three and a half days of assessment!

Figures 5.6 and 5.7 show the results of the sixteen-year follow-up. In Fig. 5.6 the "gap" in prediction has narrowed considerably. This reflects the fact that the longer one stays in an organization, the more likely one is to be promoted. The promotion is simply based on this longevity. Douglas Bray, the originator of the AT&T study (Bray 1978), has called the results in Fig. 5.6 evidence of the "upward creep of turkeys." The data in Fig. 5.7 show that "turkeys" can creep only so far, however. By shifting the focus to *fourth*-level management, the "gap" reappears. Here it can be seen that

		Predicted to reach third-level (middle) management		
		Yes	No	
Results: Did they make middle management?	Yes	39	20	59
	No	22	42	64
		61	62	123

Fig. 5.5 *Results of AT&T assessment center predictions concerning newcomers' future attainment of third-level management positions: eight years later. (Adapted from D. W. Bray, R. J. Campbell, and D. L. Grant, 1974,* Formative Years in Business, *p. 69. Copyright © 1974 by John Wiley & Sons, Inc. Reprinted by permission of John Wiley & Sons, Inc.)*

		Predicted to reach third-level (middle) management		
		Yes	No	
Results: Did they make middle management?	Yes	48	37	85
	No	6	19	25
		54	56	110

Fig. 5.6 *Results of the AT&T assessment center predictions concerning newcomers' future attainment of third-level management positions: sixteen years later. (From D. W. Bray, 1978, The AT&T assessment center program. Talk given at the annual meeting of the Academy of Management Association, San Francisco.)*

25/54 = 46 percent of those predicted to reach the third level in ten years actually made the fourth level in sixteen years. In contrast, only 10/56 = 18 percent of those predicted *not* to reach the third level actually made it all the way to the fourth level.

These results from AT&T clearly show that their assessment center was able to identify managerial talent among new employees upon their entry into the organization. The predictions were not 100 percent "fool-

	Predicted to reach third-level of management		
	Yes	No	
Results: Did they make it to the fourth-level of management? Yes	25	10	35
No	29	46	75
	54	56	110

Fig. 5.7 *Results of the AT&T assessment center predictions concerning newcomers' future attainment of fourth-level management positions: sixteen years later. (From D. W. Bray, 1978. The AT&T Assessment center program. Talk given at the annual meeting of the Academy of Management Association, San Francisco.)*

proof," but they show the power of this approach to managerial selection. Figure 5.8 shows the type of psychological jargon used by psychologists when referring to the "hits and misses" of predictions made during organizational selection.

		Prediction	
		Success	Failure
Results	Success	True positive (correct prediction)	False negative
	Failure	False positive	True negative (correct prediction)

Fig. 5.8 *Types of outcomes from organization selection procedures.*

Referring back to Fig. 5.5, it can be seen that the assessment center predictions were *incorrect* $(20 + 22)/123 = 34$ percent of the time. Is this a "high" rate? What might account for these "misses" in prediction? Chapter 6 on socialization will give a detailed explanation of what caused these prediction errors. In brief, the most appealing explanation is that the assessors could not possibly anticipate the *type of job environment* that the newcomers would be placed in. It is certainly possible for a person of high potential to fail if put into a work environment of very low challenge. It is also possible that a lower potential person might develop managerial skills when put into a job environment of high challenge. *This is precisely what was found at AT&T.* The subject is discussed further in Chapter 6 as a topic in postentry socialization.

Given these positive results it is no wonder that AT&T has now assessed over 200,000 persons for a variety of managerial and technical jobs. In 1977, for example, 18,000 persons were assessed, but 30,000 were assessed in 1978—a clearly increasing trend (Bray 1978).

A concluding note of caution. Despite the current (*and increasing*) popularity of the assessment center method, there are some researchers who have called for some degree of caution in "jumping on the assessment center bandwagon." (See for example, Hinrichs 1978; Howard 1974; Klimoski and Strickland 1977). Four concerns have been expressed. The first concern is that some studies of the assessment center method have not followed the sound scientific principles evidenced in the AT&T study that was just described. One departure from the AT&T design is to use an assessment center to make hiring decisions without first having hired both high- *and low-*rated people. Unless the low-rated persons are also hired and monitored, an organization cannot assess the true validity of a selection procedure. A second disturbing departure from the AT&T design is that some organizations disclose the results of the assessment center to line management. This easily creates a *self-fulfilling prophecy,* making the assessment center predictions appear to be better than they really are.

A second concern is that too few organizations have actually conducted validity studies of the kind done at AT&T. Most validity studies seem to come from a few corporate giants, e.g., AT&T, IBM, SOHIO, and Union Carbide. It appears that smaller companies have accepted the assessment center method without conducting studies of their own.

The third area of concern is related to the second. It is that very few research studies have been published since 1972 (Klimoski and Strickland 1977). This obviously reflects a general acceptance of the assessment center method, but some may view it as a dangerous trend.

The fourth concern is that most assessment center predictions have been compared with (i.e., validated against) either future salary or promotions, rather than with measures of actual job performance. Because today's assessors are managers from the organizations themselves, they are undoubtedly quite familiar with pay and promotional policies. It is thus possible that the assessment center predictions are only a duplication of the already existing procedure for deciding on promotions from within. If this turns out to be true, the high cost of assessment ($200–1,000 per person) may not be warranted.

ASSESSMENT CENTERS AND REALISTIC RECRUITMENT

Given the four concerns just raised, it appears that the 90 studies done (Klimoski and Strickland 1977) of assessment center predictions are still insufficient to conclude beyond most reasonable doubts that the assessment center method is *the* superior method for future organizational selection decisions. What else might be added to the list of concerns about assessment centers?

It seems clear to this author that future studies of assessment centers *must* also consider their impact on the job survival of newcomers. Since the centers try to condense important organizational realities into meaningful exercises, the assessment center method also communicates information to job candidates about what to expect if they are hired or promoted into the job. On the surface it seems as if this method combines the best of *both* realistic recruitment and accurate selection of newcomers. It is unfortunate, however, that we do *not* have data about the impact of assessment centers on the creation of realistic expectations and reduction of voluntary turnover. This is a clear and important next step in our understanding of assessment centers.

Despite this obvious enthusiasm, we should probably not expect too much from research on the recruiting versus selecting effects of assessment centers because they are concerned almost exclusively with *job*-related experiences. Thus they probably do a good job of creating realistic *job* expectations, but do not usually address other types of expectations that would normally be included in realistic recruitment. These would include information on all other nontask- or job-related organizational conditions. Thus the assessment center is not a complete substitute for realistic recruitment, but it appears to be a welcome addition—one that is complementary to realistic recruitment.

THE UTILITY OF A SELECTION PROCEDURE

Selection procedures can be evaluated in terms of the *utility,* or usefulness to the organization. The concept of utility involves a comparison between the accuracy of one selection procedure and another (or using none at all). It is a concept of *incremental advantage.* In some cases the comparison is between using a new test and using an existing one. In others it may be the more basic issue of assessing how much a procedure improves predictions, compared with using no systematic method at all.

The factors that influence selection procedure utility are shown in Fig. 5.9. The three most immediate effects on utility (test validity, selection ratio, and precentage of presently successful employees) will be discussed here. Predictor and criterion reliability have a direct effect on test validity. Without reliable measures of each, it's nearly impossible to obtain a high validity (i.e., correlation) between them.

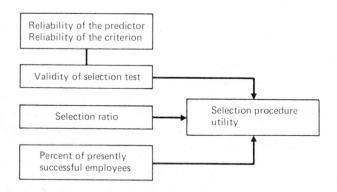

Fig. 5.9 *Factors influencing selection procedure utility.*

Validity. Test validity has a positive effect on test utility, i.e., the higher the validity, the higher the utility. Thus if a new selection procedure (e.g., a test) has a higher validity than present methods, it is of greater utility to the organization (assuming that no other factors are changed). Figure 5.10 shows graphically why this is true.

The only difference between illustrations (a) and (b) in the figure is that test validity is about $r = .00$ in (a) and about $r = .65$ in (b). The difference in scatterplots shows this difference in test validity. The circular

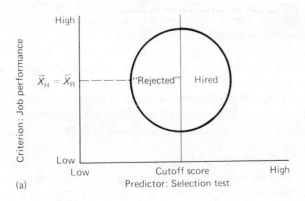

(a)

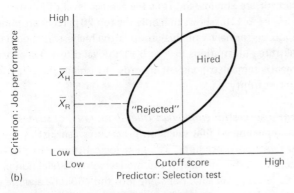

(b)

$\bar{X}_H$ = mean job performance of those "hired"
$\bar{X}_R$ = mean job performance of those "rejected"

Fig. 5.10 *Effects of validity on utility.*

shape of (a) shows there is no relationship between test score and job performance, whereas in (b) there is clearly a positive relationship.

Figure 5.10(a) shows that the average job performance of those "hired"[6] is equal to that of those who are "rejected." In Fig. 5.10(b) there

---

[6] An axiom of the test validation procedure is that *all* job candidates, even those with low scores, are hired during the validation period. This is necessary to find out the true relationship between test score and job performance. Therefore, "rejected" is in quotes to represent the fact that this is what the selection decisions will be for *future* job candidates *after* the period of test validation.

is a clear difference between the two groups. Therefore, the higher validity of the test in (b) means higher utility to the organization, since better job performers *on the average* are hired.

Selection ratio. The selection ratio (SR) is the percentage of job applicants who are actually hired, so that a *low* SR means *few* persons are hired from those who apply. As the SR goes *down,* the utility of a selection procedure goes *up.* That is, the "more selective" an organization becomes, the more useful is the particular selection procedure. Figure 5.11 shows this graphically.

Figure 5.11(a) shows that all those who apply for a job are hired, a situation more common than most people realize. Thus the average job performance of those hired ($\overline{X}_H$) is shown to be moderate. Figure 5.11(b) shows that 80 percent of those who apply are hired, with the result that the lowest 20 percent are eliminated. Thus the average level of job performance goes up. Figure 5.11(c) shows that only the top 20 percent are hired, and the average job performance of this group is the highest. It should be noted that in the three illustrations in Fig. 5.11 the validity between test and job performance remained constant in order to isolate the effect of changes in SR on test utility.

Percent of presently successful employees (the "base rate" of success). It should always be remembered that selection procedures can just as easily be thought of as *rejection* procedures. The next logical step is for the organization to decide whether it's worth the money to put a selection procedure in place to reject applicants. For some jobs this could be a waste of time and money *if* most people hired can perform the job successfully. Hence the concept of *percent of presently successful employees* becomes relevant for utility analysis. If this percentage is very high, there is serious doubt about the need for a selection procedure to reject those few candidates unfit to do the job. (The most likely explanation is that the particular job is a relatively simple one that most people could perform adequately.)

The organization must compare two percentages: the percentage of presently successful employees using present methods and the percentage of employees who are successful when a new selection method is used. If the new method yields a sufficiently higher percentage, it increases the utility of the selection procedure. This is likely to occur when the percentage of presently successful employees is *low* to begin with because it's

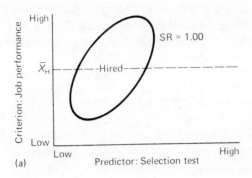

(a)

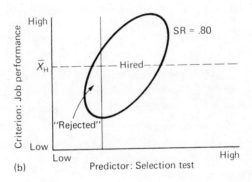

(b)

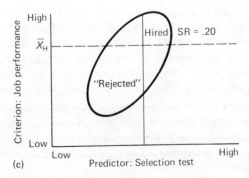

(c)

$\overline{X}_H$ = mean job performance of those "hired"

Fig. 5.11 *Effects of selection ratio on utility.*

easier to make an improvement. This is illustrated in Fig. 5.5 with the actual results from AT&T's assessment center method, as shown earlier. If the assessment center were *not* used, the percent of successful employees hired would be 48 percent (20 + 39 divided by 123). When the center was used, the percentage of successful hires went up to 64 percent (39 divided by 39 + 22). The difference between these two percentages (64 versus 48 percent) shows the *increase in utility* to AT&T created by the assessment center.

This brings us back to the original question of how the percentage of presently successful employees affects the utility of a selection procedure. The *lower* this percentage, the greater the utility will be for a new selection technique. If the base rate is already high, it's unlikely that much greater selection accuracy will be gained from a new procedure.

CONCLUSIONS

1. Job analysis methods are used to determine the hiring needs of organizations. There is a wide range of techniques that can be used to do a job analysis, e.g., observation, interviews, questionnaires, etc.

2. There are two fundamental approaches to job analysis: job requirements and worker rewards. The former affects the match between abilities and job requirements, and the latter affects the match between needs and the organizational climates.

3. There are three types of selection tests: aptitude, achievement, and motivation. Aptitude tests are those most often used in selection, with moderate success. Motivation tests are poor predictors of job performance, although they do predict which occupations will be entered and how satisfied people will be in those occupations. Achievement tests (particularly work samples and simulations of job conditions) are increasing in popularity.

4. Using the best tests available results in correlations of about .35 between the test score and future job performance (.45 if the test predicts success during training). Whether this is high or low depends on many factors in the specific situation, e.g., the size of a sample in a test validity study.

5. Interviews for selection purposes are notoriously poor predictors of future job performance; yet they continue to be universally used.

Interviews are, however, a good way to obtain facts about a job candidate's background and work history. This type of information may be predictive of job performance.

6. The assessment center technique, made popular by AT&T, combines several different ways to assess job candidates under the close watch of trained observers. This method has been quite successful in predicting future job behavior, e.g., as far as eight and sixteen years in the future.

7. The assessment center also appears to create realistic job expectations for candidates, but this impact has not been studied. The method appears promising as both a means of selection and of realistic recruitment.

8. The utility of a selection procedure is enhanced by high test validity, a low selection ratio, and a small percentage of employees who are presently successful (i.e., a low base rate).

Socialization of Newcomers

6

The focus of this chapter is on the immediate postentry period of newcomers to organizations. First socialization is defined, second the basic strategies employed by organizations to socialize newcomers are described, and last the psychological processes by which newcomers get committed to organizations are discussed. Several authors have condensed the common elements among newcomers experiences in diverse organizations into *stage models* of socialization. Four stage models are reviewed here, and an overall, integrative model is constructed that captures the most typical events for newcomers to organizations. Finally, case studies are described in detail to illustrate the stages of socialization. The examples include MBA students at two "leading" graduate business schools, police recruits, AT&T managers, and army recruits in basic training.

Socialization is then linked to the selection process. Depending on the *type of organization,* selection and socialization may be used as substitute ways to match individuals with organizations. The topic of "matching" concludes this chapter. The studies that directly examine the effects of matching person to organization are described, and the possibility of negative "side effects" from a too successful matching process is considered.

WHAT IS ORGANIZATIONAL SOCIALIZATION?

A central theme throughout this book has been the matching of person and organization, running through the topics of realistic recruitment, organizational choice, and the selection of newcomers. Over 25 years ago, Bakke (1953) described the *fusion process* of matching person and organization as composed of (1) the organization's *socialization* of the newcomer, and (2) the newcomer's *personalizing* of the organization.

Over the years, much more has been written about socialization than has been written about the personalizing process (e.g., Brim and Wheeler 1966; Schein 1968, 1978; Van Maanen 1976a). There are some good reasons why the socializing function has received more attention than has the personalizing function. First, in most organizations newcomers enter alone or in small numbers. They enter an ongoing system in which they tend to be overwhelmed by the inertia and traditions of the organization, and by the sheer numbers of established insiders. Thus it's much easier to observe how newcomers change than it is to detect changes in the organization caused by newcomers. Second, the "unit of analysis" is clear when examining socialization of individuals, but harder to define in the case of individuals personalizing organizations. That is, if one wants to see how newcomers get socialized, it's relatively easy to define the target group for study. However, if one wants to assess "personalizing changes" in the organization caused by newcomers, where should one look? The problem is one of defining what is meant by "the organization" since the organization could be a work group, department, division, or the entire legal corporate entity.

Targets of Socialization

Once socialization has been defined as those changes caused by the organization that take place in newcomers, it is easy to see that socialization is an extremely broad topic. One way to grasp this topic is to view the newcomer's effectiveness at work as determined by three factors: (1) accurate *knowledge* of what is expected, i.e., clarity, not ambiguity, about one's role in that organization, (2) the appropriate *skills and abilities* to do the job, and (3) the *motivation* to do at least the minimum acceptable performance. Examples of organizational influence on role expectations are job descriptions, formal instructions, and a variety of informal communications from peers, subordinates, and one's own boss. If organizational selection procedures do not supply the organization with newcomers who are qualified for jobs, various types of job-skill training programs are used to increase the degree of matching between abilities and job requirements. [See Goldstein (1976) for a discussion of skill training.] Finally, if selection via motivation tests and/or the use of realistic recruitment does not ensure sufficiently high motivation, organizations may resort to the use of: (1) overt indoctrination attempts (2) subtle "seduction" techniques (discussed later in this chapter), (3) compensation systems (see Lawler 1971), (4) job enrichment (see Hackman and Oldham 1980), and (5) participative management (see Marrow, Bowers, and Seashore 1967) to motivate newcomers along channels desired by the organization. The first two of these are discussed here; the remaining three have already been the topic of entire books.

Types of Socialization Strategies

Five "pure" types of socialization strategies have been used, although in any particular organization there is likely to be a "mix" of them. The first is _training_, which may be done on either a full- or part-time basis. Training refers to the acquisition of skills and/or knowledge related to one's job performance. Schein (1964) has distinguished between two variations of part-time training, i.e., training-while-working and working-while-training. This simply places the correct emphasis on either work or training. In the former case, the newcomer is assigned to a "regular" department and in the latter the primary responsibility is with the training department even though the newcomer is placed in another department, and may rotate among departments.

A second socialization strategy is to _educate_ newcomers to the various policies, procedures, norms, etc. of the organization. Although this education is often combined with skill training, there are examples where education exists as a pure type without a focus on actual job skills. Some companies have designed socialization experiences of this type as a means of smoothing the entry of "hard-core unemployed" persons into an active, productive role in the organization. [See Salipante and Goodman (1976) for an evaluation of these educational programs.] A third type of strategy is _apprenticeship_, which actually contains equal elements of both training and education. This involves a one-on-one relationship between the newcomer and an insider who has the responsibility both to train _and_ to educate the newcomer. The example of a New England bank studied by both Argyris (1954) and Alderfer (1971) is a good one in which all new management trainees were assigned a "big brother" for the 33 weeks of their development program. Another good, current example is how most Ph.D.'s are trained today in graduate schools. Most doctoral candidates work quite closely with their "major professor," and particularly so in the last year while doing their dissertations.

A fourth category is called *debasement experiences*. The purpose here is to "unfreeze" or "unhinge" the newcomer from previously held beliefs and values, and to humble the person so that a new self-image can be developed by the organization. Schein (1964) has identified two types of debasement experiences—"sink-or-swim" and the "upending experience." The *sink-or-swim* ploy is designed to humble the newcomer by assigning a job to be done, but then giving very little definition to the task or the amount of authority the newcomer has, and giving relatively little support. The *upending experience* is designed to alter the newcomer's expectations and self-image in a dramatic way. This can take one of two forms: (1) put the newcomer in a situation in which early failure is guaranteed, or (2) put the newcomer in a position of very menial responsibility. In either case the confidence of the newcomer is shaken, so that the organization is in a better position to exert influence.

The fifth, and final, type is much more subtle than a debasement experience: it is the attempt to socialize the newcomer via *cooptation* or *seduction*. Cooptation is a two-step strategy. First, the newcomer is admitted to the organization, and then is "absorbed" into it. Cooptation works best when newcomers enter singly, rather than in a group. Organizational "seduction" of newcomers is a slightly different version of subtle socialization. The crux of the seduction process is to present the newcomer with a number of "tempting choices." The *illusion* of a choice is maintained, but in fact one alternative is more attractive than the others (Lewicki 1978). The postchoice rationalization process (Aronson 1972; Festinger 1957) thus favors the organization's viewpoint, as the newcomer rationalizes the wisdom of decisions made. For example, new Ph.D.'s working as assistant professors often feel tension between commitment to the university or to their chosen profession because they are constantly having to make choices about how they spend their time. Universities rarely confront assistant professors with such explicit choices. Rather, they influence the professors' decisions via the reward structure, e.g., curtailing funds for travel, but providing released time from teaching to develop new courses. By influencing decisions in this way, universities create the illusion that assistant professors control their own destinies.

The Psychology of Socialization

In this section, the psychological mechanisms that cause *internal* changes in attitudes and commitment to an organization are explored. The work of Lewicki (1978) and Schein (1968) has been particularly helpful in understanding this process.

Effective socialization usually means that the newcomer has changed some basic attitudes and beliefs. Effective socialization thus means an *internal commitment* to the organization, rather than just compliance with organization practices. At the basis, then, of the socialization process is the need to understand how people's attitudes change.

One method is to have the newcomers expend a lot of time, effort, and energy. A dependable consequence of energy expenditure is the enhanced attractiveness of the object of this effort (Lewis 1965). The reason this occurs is that individuals need to rationalize (or justify) the choices they make (Aronson 1972). The primary danger of this strategy is that the newcomer will come to expect something in return. Thus most organizations couple the inducement of effort expenditure with two forms of "payoffs": (1) the conferring of status, and (2) the giving of "plentiful hygiene factors" (Lewicki 1978). In both these cases, the "payoffs" tend to arouse in the newcomer feelings of *obligation* that lead to further commitment to the new organization.

Organizations achieve high status themselves in a variety of ways. They can be market leaders in a particular segment of the economy. They can employ high-status members, whose status "rubs off" onto the rest of the organization. They can make entry difficult. They can give rewards that are unique to themselves and not available elsewhere. Finally, they can live off past status.

The conferring of status can be done in a wide variety of ways. Some organizations confer status on newcomers immediately upon their entry in the form of a "one of the chosen few" message. Even if the organization sends such a message to the newcomer, the message does not necessarily mean that this person is a fully accepted insider. There may still be a well-defined internal status hierarchy, and the newcomer ("one of a chosen few") is still at the bottom. For example, some Ivy League colleges are rather adept at simultaneously sending these (apparently conflicting) messages to college entrants. On the one hand there is the message of elitism ("you are one of the chosen few"), but on the other hand there is the message that you still may be unworthy. This is a form of guilt arousal. That is, the organization communicates to the newcomer that it has taken some risk in admitting him or her, and wants the newcomer to know it. The newcomer's resulting gratitude is then used by the organization as the basis for future commitment.

A second type of payoff for effort expenditure is what Lewicki (1978) calls the supply of PLUSH—a *Pl*entiful *U*nlimited *S*upply of *H*ygienes.[1] Examples of "PLUSHness" abound: (1) generous photocopying, telephone, and expense budgets, (2) good secretarial service, (3) free recreational facilities or tickets to events, (4) convenient parking facilities, (5) "flexibility" in using office staff and equipment to conduct personal business (Lewicki 1978). All of these, plus the normal fringe benefits, are what has been called *system rewards* (Katz and Kahn 1966) because they are designed to reward *membership in the system* rather than one's job performance, per se. These PLUSH (system) rewards do not directly build internal commitment to the organization, because the newcomer can always justify the decision to remain employed in terms of the PLUSHness of the environment. They do, however, create feelings of *obligation* that can be used to initiate a more subtle form of internal commitment.

By feeling a sense of obligation, newcomers are in a position in which they may be *seduced* by the organization (Lewicki 1978). The seduction process has several elements.

- The individual is induced to make "tempting choices," i.e., there appear to be at least two alternatives, but one of them is clearly more positive than the others. For example, a professor may be given a "choice" either to work on internal affairs of the university (teaching and committees, or to work on external affairs (research or travel).

- Enticement, not force, is used to influence newcomers. That is, promises and opportunities are used rather than threats or punishments.

- The intention of the seducer is not only to entice the person to do something but often to draw the individual away from "principles" as well. It is often an attempt to change the newcomer's values as well as the newcomer's behavior, i.e., it is aimed at building commitment, not just getting compliance.

---

[1] Hygiene factors (Herzberg 1968) refer to things such as salary, working conditions, status, security, supervision, peer relationships, and company policies. They are all those factors other than the actual task or work itself.

- The "appearance of a choice" is crucial to the process. Even though the individual may be subject to much inducement (e.g., promises or flattery), the person is always "theoretically free" to say *no*. The significance of this is that the important *internal* changes in a person's beliefs and values occur *after* decisions are made. This is called *post-decisional justification*, i.e., individuals need to *feel* rational, and will alter their beliefs to conform to their behavior.

The seduction process (Lewicki 1978) is one of getting newcomers to make "decisions" such as outlined above. The building of internal commitment is the *consequence* of these decisions because newcomers justify their choices in terms of their commitment to the organization.

STAGES OF SOCIALIZATION

This section traces the similarities among various forms of socialization as a series of *stages*. The concept of a *stage model* is quite popular throughout the social and behavioral sciences. In economics, there are models of how developing countries grow into "fully" industrialized economies. In psychology, there are stage models that describe the growth of one's personality. In vocational psychology, career stages have been an important concern. Stages of the growth of a small group have been studied in social psychology. The stages through which organizations pass during "organizational development" have been the concern of organizational psychologists. Thus it's hardly surprising that those interested in organizational socialization also view this process as proceeding through several stages.

There are probably three crucial questions a stage model must answer if it is to be useful in understanding a process as complicated as organizational socialization. The first, and most basic, is to define the stages composing the model. This is not as easy as it might seem since there are two basic ways to go about doing this: (1) stages may be based on the passage of time, or (2) stages may be based on the occurrence of certain events. These are not completely separate ways of defining stages, however. For example, in order for several events to have happened, some time must elapse. On the other hand, the mere passage of time does not guarantee that certain crucial events will have occurred. It is for this reason that *events* are chosen as the better way to define organizational socialization. The events composing each stage should be *homogeneous within* that stage.

That is, they should have more in common with other events of a particular stage than with events in different stages.

A second question that a stage model should answer is how the stages are related to one another. If there is a sequence among stages, it should be spelled out, e.g., the *direction* of movement from stage to stage should be clear. The third, and final, question that must be addressed concerns what accounts for movement from one stage to another. Another way to put this is how does one know that movement has taken place, e.g., how would either the newcomer or the organization know that the "final" stage of socialization has been successfully reached.

Before developing a single comprehensive model of the stages in socialization, four recent and well-known stage models will be presented. There are several themes common to all four stage models. First, each is defined in terms of the individual's view during socialization, rather than that of the organization. This is consistent with the view that the direction of influence runs from the organization to the individual in the case of socialization, but goes the other way in the personalizing process. Second, each of the models includes a preentry stage. These will be briefly mentioned, but have been extensively covered earlier in this book. Third, the respective definitions of stages are rather broad, and are defined somewhat differently across the four examples. Fourth, these stage models are primarily based upon events that occur, rather than just upon the passage of time.

Feldman's three-stage entry model. Feldman (1976a, 1976b) proposed a three-stage model of organizational entry and socialization based on his analysis of the previously published research literature and on his study of newly hired hospital employees.[2]

Stage 1: *Anticipatory Socialization: "Getting In"*

Two events occur in this stage. One is the degree to which the expectations of both individuals and organizations are realistic. The second concerns the degree to which the newcomer is well matched in both senses of the Matching Model. The more realistic the expectations and the higher the congruence between newcomer and organization, the easier will be the transition from outsider to insider.

---

[2] One finding from the hospital employee data is worthy of note here. There was a strong, positive relationship ($r = .60$) between how well newcomers were matched (in needs satisfaction) to the organization and their satisfaction with working at the hospital. This is exactly what the Matching Model stipulates.

Stage 2: *Accommodation: "Breaking In"*

Four events compose this postentry stage. The first is being initiated to one's job. An individual's abilities to do a good job have a strong influence on the initial level of the newcomer's self-esteem. Second, the newcomer is typically initiated into a group of fellow employees and begins to establish new interpersonal relationships. The primary indicator of success here is how well the newcomer is accepted. Third, the full definition of the newcomer's role in the organization begins to unfold. For example, the degree to which one can make effective use of one's time, and the degree to which one can deviate from strict organizational policy are two examples of learning how things "really" work on the inside. The last event in this stage concerns the degree to which one's self-evaluation of work performance is congruent with that of the organization. The first formal evaluation of job performance can easily be viewed as the termination of "breaking in."

Stage 3: *Role Management: "Settling In"*

The final stage is typified by the resolution of two conflicts that inevitably crop up. The first is how work in the new organization fits in with one's life interests outside of work. The second is how the newcomer resolves all the varieties of conflict at the work place itself.

Buchanan's three-stage early career model. Buchanan (1974) studied new managers from five governmental agencies and three large manufacturing concerns. His objective in this research was to study the level of one's *commitment* to a new organization as influenced by early socialization experiences. This stage model differs from Feldman's in the sense that it is concerned only with postentry events, and because it covers a much longer span of one's early work career.

Stage 1: *First Year: Basic Training and Initiation*

The first year on the job is characterized by a focus on the security and existence needs of the newcomer. The first event is the establishment of role clarity by the newcomer. It is similar to Feldman's Stage 1. The second is the establishment of cohesion within one's peer group—an event similar to Feldman's view that newcomers must be accepted by their own work group. Third is the relationship of one's immediate peer group to the rest of the organization, *that is, the extent to which it is in harmony or conflict with other parts of the organization. Fourth, Buchanan discusses the degree to which expectations are realized, and the possibility of reality shock when they are not. Fifth, the degree to which the new job provides a challenge to the employee was found to be crucial for new AT&T managers (Berlew and Hall 1966), and is included by Buchanan as well. Finally, he goes so far as to include loyalty conflicts, both within the organization and between the organization and outside interests. In contrast, Feldman had put the resolution of these conflicts in a later stage.*

Stage 2: *Performance: Years Two, Three, and Four at Work*

Buchanan's second career stage concerns the achievement or growth needs of newcomers. There are five events that define this particular stage. First, the degree to which one feels personally important is crucial for long-run commitment to the new organization. Closely related to this is a second factor—the extent to which the new organization reinforces one's self-image. Third, the newcomer must come to terms with the internal conflict between needs for achievement and the fear of failure. Finally, at this stage newcomers will be sensitive to organizational norms *regarding commitment and loyalty. The issue of the newcomer's future internal mobility may rest on the degree to which the newcomer can adopt the desired degree of loyalty.*

Stage 3: *Organizational Dependability: The Fifth Year and Beyond*

Buchanan chose to lump all succeeding years into this stage since he believes that later events are much harder to predict than earlier ones. In essence, Stages 1 and 2 contain events that are common for most newcomers. By Stage 3, however, quite a lot of diversity occurs that makes it much harder to identify any particular set of experiences as typical for this group of insiders.

Porter–Lawler–Hackman three-stage entry model. Porter, Lawler, and Hackman (1975) base their stage model on a review of research conducted by others in contrast to the first two stage models that grew out of a research study conducted by each author.

Stage 1: *Prearrival*

The major event of this stage concerns the newcomer's personal values (or desires) and expectations. The degree to which these are subsequently matched to reality (in the next stage) is considered a crucial event. The second event of this stage is the degree to which the newcomer was actively recruited by the organization compared with those who worked very hard to convince the organization they should be hired.

Stage 2: *Encounter*

At the point of entry into the new organization, the emergence of discrepancies begins between (1) expectations and reality and (2) values (human needs) and reality. The authors point out that the organization responds to the newcomer in three ways: reinforcement, nonreinforcement, and punishment. These three reactions can be intentional, or completely unplanned. Reinforcement is provided to those facets of the newcomer that are confirmed and valued by the new organization. Nonreinforcement is shown by ignoring certain characteristics of the newcomer. Finally, punishment is meted out to the newcomer who engages in behaviors that the organization actively discourages, such as joining a union at Texas Instruments. [See Nissen (1978) for an account.]

Stage 3: *Change and Acquisition*

Borrowing from Caplow (1964), the authors list four areas of change for newcomers. First, the newcomer's self-image is altered. This depends on the age and previous working experience of the newcomer. The younger and less experienced someone is, the greater the change in self-image during socialization. Second, new relationships are formed. Third, new values are adopted. Fourth, new behaviors are acquired.

Schein's three-stage socialization model. In a recent book on careers, Schein (1978) develops a three-stage model of entry–socialization–mutual acceptance to describe the sequence of events that confront the typical newcomer to an organization. The second two stages are relevant for this discussion of postentry experiences. Schein's view of these events is particularly appealing for two reasons. First, he has adopted the distinction between individual and organizational perspectives used throughout this book. Second, he goes into greater detail than some others in describing the flow of events from both these viewpoints.

Stage 1: *Entry*

Schein identifies four "problems" that confront both the individual and the organization during this stage. The first is "obtaining accurate information in a climate of mutual selling" *(1978, p. 85)*. In Chapter 2 there was a detailed discussion of the four conflicts that occur during "traditional" recruitment and selection practices (see Fig. 2.1). Second, there is a mutual problem of creating false expectations about the early part of the newcomer's career in the organization. Both parties tend to focus on long-term matches, but may overlook the fact that the responsibilities encountered in early months or years may be quite different from later job responsibilities. Third, recruitment practices often build incorrect images of the organization, as discussed and documented at length in Chapters 2 and 3. Fourth, the organizational choices made by job candidates cannot be optimal when they are based on biased or deficient information, as discussed in Chapter 4.

Stage 2: *Socialization*

During the postentry period, both the individual and the organization face difficult issues. From the individual's viewpoint, five "tasks" (to use Schein's term) must be tackled. First, the newcomer must accept the reality of the human organization. The difficulties of learning to work with others were often underestimated by the managers Schein studied. Second, newcomers must learn how to deal with resistance to change, i.e., good ideas are not always accepted. Third, newcomers must learn "how to work" in their particular job. This may mean coping with either too much or too little organizational structure, and too much or too little job definition. Fourth, the difficult tasks of learning to work with one's own boss and comprehending the "real" working of the organizational reward system also confront the newcomer. Two key issues with respect to the newcomer's boss concern the degree of trust–mistrust, and independence-dependence. The final task is for the newcomer to locate his or her "place" in the organization and to develop an identity around it.

From the organization's viewpoint, three basic issues underlie the assessment of the newcomer. First, will this person fit into the organization, i.e., will there be a congruence between the needs and personality of the newcomer and the present climate of the organization?

Second, will the newcomer be able to be an innovative contributor to the organization? Finally, will the newcomer be able to learn and grow throughout a career in this particular organization?

Stage 3: Mutual Acceptance

This is the major transition from newcomer to insider. Schein has done a fine job of describing the "signals" that individuals and organizations send to each other to communicate mutual acceptance. Organizations send six types of signals to newcomers indicating acceptance (1) a positive performance appraisal, (2) a salary increase, (3) a new job assignment, (4) organizational secrets are shared, e.g., how things "really" work, what "really" happened in the past, and how others evaluate the new person, (5) initiation rites confirm the passage to a new status, e.g., a party or the granting of a special privilege, and (6) actual promotion. This last one is often the only one that some employees trust, yet this is surely not the only way organizations signal acceptance.

Newcomers also send signals which indicate they accept the new organization. The most obvious of these is not quitting. However, the mere fact that a newcomer elects to remain does not necessarily mean he or she has accepted the organization or feels any commitment to it. A second category of signals includes all the indications that the newcomer is highly motivated, for example, working long hours, doing extra tasks, and being enthusiastic about work. Since some newcomers may be highly involved with their work (and not with the organization), this high work motivation may sometimes be misread as commitment to the organization. The organization must try to distinguish between loyalties felt toward the work itself and those felt toward the organization. The last category includes the acceptance of doing undesirable work, tolerating delays, and putting up with organizational "red tape." The most common case is for the newcomer to accept a temporary starting position with little challenge and responsibility in order to attain a much different job after "paying one's dues."

An integrative approach to stages of socialization. Table 6.1 combines all four of these models into a single, integrated view of postentry organizational socialization. The first three stages refer to the socialization process

TABLE 6.1

Stages in the socialization process

Stage 1: Confronting and accepting organizational reality

  a) Confirmation/disconfirmation of expectations
  b) Conflicts between personal values and needs, and the organizational climates
  c) Discovering which aspects of oneself that are reinforced, not reinforced, and which that are punished by the organization.

Stage 2: Achieving role clarity

  a) Being initiated to the tasks in the new job
  b) Defining one's interpersonal roles
    i) with respect to peers
    ii) with respect to one's boss
  c) Learning to cope with resistance to change
  d) Congruence between one's own evaluation of performance and the organization's evaluation of performance
  e) Learning how to work within the given degree of structure and ambiguity.

Stage 3: Locating oneself in the organizational context

  a) Learning which modes of one's own behavior are congruent with those of the organization
  b) Resolution of conflicts at work, and between outside interests and work
  c) Commitment to work and to the organization stimulated by first-year job challenge
  d) The establishment of an altered self-image, new interpersonal relationships, and the adoption of new values.

Stage 4: Detecting signposts of successful socialization

  a) Achievement of organizational dependability and commitment
  b) High satisfaction in general
  c) Feelings of mutual acceptance
  d) Job involvement and internal work motivation
  e) The sending of "signals" between newcomers and the organization to indicate mutual acceptance.

proper and the final stage exemplifies the transition from newcomer to insider. It would be wise at this point to study the events of each stage since this comprehensive model will be used to interpret the events of several case studies from rather diverse organizations.

THE DYNAMICS OF ORGANIZATIONAL SOCIALIZATION

Socialization of students. Accounts of MBA student socialization are available for the Harvard (Cohen 1973) and M.I.T. (Schein 1967) graduate schools of business administration. Cohen's (1973) *Gospel According to the Harvard Business School* was a best-seller several years ago. In between anecdotal accounts of various classmates, Cohen gives an excellent first-hand description of organizational life for the MBA student at the HBS. The first year at the HBS is quite highly regimented, in contrast to the first year at other schools. It is a "lockstep" program in which all first-year students take the same courses in the same sequence.

Prior to their arrival in the fall, incoming students are sent a package of course reading material. Upon arrival, they discover that the first examination will be Saturday morning at the end of the *first* week.

There are other examples of HBS's attempt to design "upending experiences" for this highly select group (776 were admitted from more than 3,000 who applied). For example, the opening ceremony for Cohen's class was held in an old gymnasium under rather primitive and crowded conditions. Each newcomer is sent a "suggested" list of materials to purchase for written classwork. The newcomer is assigned to a "section" (Cohen's had 94 students), which takes all classes together for the entire first year. Whatever feelings of elitism that may have existed on arrival in Boston tend to evaporate with this kind of treatment. Completing these "entry shock" experiences is an incredibly tight schedule, which includes four and a half classroom hours per day, all five days a week (about double the typical amount). The students are assigned an average of three cases *a day* (100 or so pages) to be read, digested, understood, and analyzed for oral discussion the next day. Written analyses of cases (WACs) are typed, put in a special large envelope, and deposited in a box for pick-up. At the precise hour of the deadline, the box is sealed and all late papers must be stacked on top of it. Late papers get a full grade lower penalty.

For the newcomer these experiences encourage the formation of "study groups" to pool resources, with the blessing of the HBS. As Cohen points out, the "illusion of belonging" is preferable to the "certainty of being on your own." Newcomers are constantly torn between feelings of competitiveness with their fellow students and the need to cooperate to survive the entry shock. As the year progresses, students increasingly know where they stand, and competition among them increases while cooperation decreases.

Newcomers learn to survive, as exemplified by picking up the "rules of the game" for "scoring points" in case discussions. Cohen describes four such strategies. First, *preventive attack* in which the student "lays out the case" for the class is desirable because one usually gets five to ten minutes of uninterrupted "air time." Second, *questioning of premises* is an attack on the original presenter. Third, the *single-point technique* is used by those who don't understand the case, or who are unprepared. It involves waiting for the correct moment when the student *does* have something to say. Fourth, *pseudo-participation* is similar to the single-point technique. One begins by making reference to the case at hand, but then quickly shifts to another point—one that is self-serving. Finally, newcomers quickly pick up the B-school jargon, e.g., "ball-park number," "to eyeball," "to massage data," "the real world," and "hobo problems" (Human Behavior in Organizations, HBO or "hobo" is a first-year course.)

The degree to which the detached, analytic case study approach was adopted by these newcomers was sharply evident by midyear. When Cohen was a student, a young professor committed suicide at midyear. There was a strong feeling of guilt among students and faculty for contributing to the pressure he was under, but Cohen believes little true emotion was actually expressed. His analysis of this tragic incident is that many newcomers had already adopted the value system of the insiders, i.e., that the suicide was a "case" for detached study and analysis.

The transition from the first to the second year marks the change in status from newcomer to insider. The atmosphere during the second year is quite different. Classes are held on a higher floor, with a better view of the Charles River and downtown Boston. The curriculum is mostly elective, rather than the required "common core" that all took in their first year. Participation in classroom case discussions is still important, but is more voluntary than mandatory as it was during the first year. Insider status does not last too long, however, since the job interview process begins at midyear.

The HBS example illustrates practically all of the events listed in the comprehensive stage model of organizational socialization. (See Fig. 6.1.) Early events dramatically show the disconfirmation of expectations, e.g., newcomers felt "special" because they were admitted to an elite school, but the "messages" they received shattered this feeling. Movement well into Stage 3 (particularly event (d)—the adoption of new values) is exemplified by the reaction of many newcomers to the young professor's suicide as "a case for analysis." The second year at HBS is a good example of the school "sending signals" (Stage 4) to the students that they are now insiders. Being able to take elective courses ("mutual influence") is also a contributing factor to another event of Stage 4 socialization—"high satisfaction."

Schein's study (1967) of attitude changes at M.I.T. does not include a richly detailed description of how students were socialized, but it does provide systematic data about the outcomes of the socialization process. He had members from four different groups complete questionnaires before and after the completion of a year at M.I.T. One group was the faculty and the other three were students, i.e., "regular" masters' degree candidates, Sloan Fellows, and executives in the ten-week program. Sloan Fellows tended to be older than the regular students, had more experience, and were members of an intensive 12-month program, whereas the regular students went through two academic years of nine months each.

Schein grouped the attitude questions as follows: (1) government-business relations, (2) labor–management relations, (3) areas of corporate responsibility, (4) superior–subordinate relationships, (5) theory of how to organize and manage, (6) general cynicism-idealism about business, (7) cynicism-idealism about how to get ahead in business, (8) faith or confidence in workers, (9) attitudes toward individual versus group incentives and decisions, and (10) attitudes toward large vs. small businesses.

The initial attitudes of the regular students were about midway between those of the executives and the faculty (executives and faculty differed widely on more than half of the ten areas). At the year's end, student attitudes, as a group, were closer to those of the faculty, however. The main reason for this shift was the *type* of faculty members these students were exposed to during their first year. At M.I.T., as in many business schools, the first-year curriculum is staffed by those professors from traditional academic disciplines such as economics, quantitative analysis, and psychology. In contrast, the second year has more courses from applied areas, e.g., business policy, production management, or marketing. Upon reanalysis of the data, it became clear that faculty from traditional disciplines differed most from the executives. Thus the shift in student attitudes can be attributed to faculty influence from those teaching in the first-year courses when the incoming students were open to influence.

Socializing police recruits. Van Maanen (1976b) relates a fascinating and detailed account of police socialization. His description is divided into four stages: (1) self-selection into police work, (2) introduction to the police organization, (3) encounter with actual police work, and (4) metamorphosis into a full-fledged "cop."

Exerpts from Van Maanen's account of this process are as follows:[3]

1. Self-selection: *In the large cities, police work attracts local, family-oriented, blue-collar or middle-class white males with military experience. . . . A cultural stereotype exists about police work—high adventure, romance, contribution to society—and this stereotype is shared by virtually all who join a police force. They also enjoy the out-of-doors, nonroutine, and masculine (that is, "machismo") aspect of the work.*

   The stretched-out screening process is a critical aspect of police socialization. From the time he fills out the application blank until he gets the telephone call of acceptance, a recruit passes through a series of events designed for one purpose: to impress him with being admitted into an "elite" organization. There is a written and physical examination, an oral board, a psychiatric interview, and a background investigation (in which an applicant's friends and relatives are questioned about the most delicate matters).

2. Introduction: *Once the recruit has "made it," the department quickly and rudely informs him that he is now a "probie." During his trial period, he can be severed from membership at any time without warning, explanation, or appeal. . . . He stands in long lines waiting to receive his departmental issues (rulebook, badge, Smith and Wesson 38-caliber revolver, ticket book, chemical mace, rosewood nightstick). He spends several hundred dollars on*

---

[3] J. Van Maanen, 1976, Rookie cops and rookie managers. *Wharton Magazine* **1**: 50–54. Reprinted by permission of The Wharton Magazine.

uniforms in a designated department store. Even the swearing-in ceremony is carried out en masse, with the words of a civil servant barely audible above the din of a busy public building. . . .

The recruit's first sustained contact with the police culture occurs at the Training Academy. . . . To be one minute late to class, to utter a careless word in formation, or to walk when he should run may earn him a "gig." And a "gig" costs an extra day of work. . . . The training staff promotes solidarity through group rewards and group punishments, interclass competition, and by cajoling the newcomers—at every opportunity—to "show some unity." . . . Under the impact of "stress" training the recruit begins to change his high opinions of the department. He learns that the formal rules and regulations are applied inconsistently. . . .

3. Encounter: *Following Academy training, a recruit is introduced to the realities and complexities of policing by a Field Training Officer (FTO), the first partner assigned to a rookie policeman. He is a veteran officer who has worked patrol for several years. . . . During the long hours on patrol with his FTO, the recruit is instructed about the "real nature" of police work. First he learns, by word and deed, about the (non) worth of his Academy preparation. . . . Indeed, the rookie discovers on his first tour of duty that he does not know how to handle an unruly drunk, how to spot a traffic violator, or even to negotiate his district's physical and social terrain. . . . At first, the squawk of the police radio transmits only meaningless static. The streets of his sector appear to be a maze through which only an expert could maneuver. So the rookie never makes a move without checking with his FTO.*

4. Metamorphosis: *As long as the recruit remains with his FTO, his socialization, both psychologically (his own identity) and sociologically (with other officers) will be incomplete. To end the stigma of "trainee" or "rookie," he must take on a patrol partnership with equal accountability. . . . There is an important irony at work. Recruits are attracted to the organization through the unrealistic expectation that the work is exciting and dramatic. But an experienced officer knows such times are few and far between. . . .*

> *The patrolman must then sit back and wait, and let his expe-*
> *riences accumulate. . . . Socialization always entails the conver-*
> *sion of fantasy to reality. For patrolmen, the reality involves a*
> *two-edged disenchantment. One edge is disenchantment with the*
> *general public, the familiar "cynical" cop: the other edge is dis-*
> *enchantment with the police system itself, the "abandoned" cop.*
> *Both develop rather quickly. . . . In most ways, the squad is a*
> *team whose members cooperate in order to project certain im-*
> *pressions. To the so-called law-abiding public, the squad wished*
> *to convey the message: "We can take care of everything." To po-*
> *tential adversaries—the "street" people—the message is "Watch*
> *your step because we can do whatever we want to you." To the*
> *department, the patrol team's message must be "All is going well,*
> *there are no problems."*

The stage Van Maanen calls "introduction" roughly corresponds to Stage 1 (confronting or accepting organizational reality). His "encounter" stage is about the equivalent of Stage 2 (achieving role clarity). His "meta-morphosis" stage is rather broad, and appears to include most of the events that compose both Stages 3 (locating oneself in the organization context) and 4 (detecting signposts of successful socialization).

Socialization of AT&T managers. The Management Progress Study at AT&T (Bray et al. 1974), discussed earlier, contains a wealth of pertinent information about factors related to the job performance of newly hired managers. When the 274 men entered the various operating companies of AT&T, there was no uniform set of procedures concerning how they should be socialized. Sometimes the primary responsibility of overseeing the progress of the newcomer was assumed by the personnel department, at other times by the newcomer's own functional area boss, and at still other times by a training supervisor. The content of these early experiences ranged from interviews with insiders to formal sessions with experienced AT&T personnel and, finally, to on-the-job discussions with the new-comer's supervisor. There were some formal management-development courses, but the major means of socializing these new managers was via slow rotation through a variety of jobs in different functional areas of the company.

Their performance was evaluated every six months, but specific feedback to the manager was sporadic. The typical newcomer could expect to be paid about 15 percent more than his or her starting salary about 18 to 24 months after entry. (Inflation was minimal at that time.)

The major focus of this study was to understand what factors significantly affected the job performance of managers. The effect of *first-year* experiences on later job performance was specifically examined. The amount of *job challenge* in the *first* year was significantly related to later job performance and salary.

Job challenge was measured by two psychologists who evaluated the tape recordings of annual interviews conducted by supervisory personnel.[4] The higher the expectations the company had for the newcomer, the more challenging the job was assumed to be. These data also confirmed the fact that "hard" goals (but not impossible ones) do lead to higher job performance, a fact repeatedly found in laboratory research (Locke 1968).

Thus the net effect of high job challenge in the newcomer's first year at work is to get him or her started in a "success cycle." Challenge in early organizational experiences seems to lead to the adoption of high work standards by newcomers, which in turn leads to high job performance itself. Early success at work, then, seems to lead to more challenging assignments, and the cycle repeats itself.

In fact, early job challenge at AT&T accounted for many of the (so-called) mistakes made in predicting job performance with the assessment center. In the previous chapter, the results of assessment center predictions were presented. One type of "error" was the *false positive,* i.e., those who were predicted to reach third-level management in eight years, but who did not. Of the 22 in this group, 14 were on jobs *without high* challenge. The high competence observed in the assessment center was never really given a chance to develop.

The second type of prediction "error" is the *false negative,* i.e., those who were predicted not to reach third-level management, but who actually did. Of the 20 in this group, 11 had high job challenge the first year. Despite their lower assessed abilities, these employees developed managerial competence through the opportunities afforded by high job challenge.

---

[4] Job challenge was a composite of four aspects of one's job environment: (1) the degree to which one's boss set a model for achievement, (2) the degree of job stimulation and challenge, (3) the degree of supervisory responsibilities, and (4) the degree to which one's job included unstructured assignments.

Considered in this context, the predictions made by the AT&T assessment center staff were even more accurate than might first appear since the assessors had no way of knowing what type of job environment each newcomer would enter. This is an excellent example of the interaction between selection and socialization.

The issue of why organizations do *not* usually place newcomers on challenging jobs has been investigated. Schein (1964) found that the typical company stereotype of college graduate recruits is that (1) they are over-ambitious and have unrealistic expectations; (2) they are too theoretical, naive, and idealistic; (3) they are immature and inexperienced; (4) they are not risk takers; and (5) they don't understand the distinction between having a good idea and being able to persuade others of its merit. Moore (1974) found that people in superior positions have much longer estimates of the "learning time" for a job than do their subordinates in that particular job. Views such as these often prevent newcomers from being placed in positions of high challenge, until after a "break-in" period. The AT&T study shows, however, that *job challenge should begin immediately,* contrary to usual corporate practice.

Army socialization: basic training. The eight-week period following induction into the army, basic training, is well known to those who have gone through it. Bourne (1967) has divided this socialization into four stages: environmental shock, engagement, period of attainment, and period of termination.

Stage One, environmental shock, begins at the reception center, where almost everyone is a stranger. One of the biggest shocks is to find oneself in the organization for *24 hours a day.* This is particularly stressful on those who have not previously lived away from home. The maximum stress, as measured physiologically by blood and urine analyses, is at its peak on Day One. It has been noted by Bourne (1967, p. 189) that the levels reached on the first day are comparable to those found "in schizophrenic patients in incipient psychosis and exceed the levels reached in other supposedly stressful situations." Clearly, this is a lot of stress!

Two factors seem to increase the degree of stress on these newcomers. First, most of the expectations of the new recurits are *dis*confirmed upon arrival. Second, the administrative processing is very time consuming, boring, and ambiguous.

The typical recruit reacts with "dazed apathy." Recruits become very dependent and tend to cling to those in authority. Finally, relatively minor events tend to be overblown in their significance, e.g., the assignment to KP duty can be seen as a catastrophe to some.[5]

After the initial period of a few days at the reception center, the recruits enter Stage 2 engagement, by being assigned to a basic training company. The next eight weeks are spent in this group.

The socialization strategy here is to strip away the newcomer's "old" identity and substitute a new one in its place. This is accomplished by the ritual haircut and wearing of uniforms. There is very little privacy. During this initial period, anxiety levels drop for two reasons. First, this is what the recruits expected, i.e., they typically do not expect the reception center process to last so long. Secondly, the recruits are now much more active.

During the first four weeks of basic training, the level of anger and resentment rises slowly in the recruits. This is because they see themselves as receiving very little in return from the army for all their sacrifices. (This is a typical danger of the strategy to build commitment via high energy expenditure.) They still feel like outsiders to the army and they are constantly reminded that their own skills are of no value to the army. This anger is directed at many targets; it is hard to vent it on a particular "villain." For those of the highest status in civilian life, the resentment during this period is most acute.

The "period of attainment," the third stage, begins during the third and fourth weeks as recruits learn how to handle weapons. The scoring of accuracy with rifles is really the first time the army has given the recruit credit for an acquired skill. During the second half of basic training, a weekend pass becomes a possibility. The incidence of upper respiratory illness diminishes dramatically during the second four weeks as compared to the first four. This in itself is reassuring to those who had been ill, since it means they will be able to complete the training on time and not be transferred to another group to make up for lost time.

The fourth stage, period of termination, begins about one week before the end of basic training. There is a definite shift to feelings of euphoria, self-confidence, and discussion of plans during their upcoming leave from the army.

---

[5] KP stands for "kitchen police," i.e., various types of jobs such as cleaning dishes, disposing of garbage, etc.

The recruits' early fears of failure in basic training are gone. They now realize that the whole experience was designed to ensure a high rate of success. In fact, there are often complaints that the experience was not "tough enough." This has been confirmed by surveys, e.g., Wiskoff's study (1977), of expectation disconfirmation in the various armed services. This disappointment stems from the fact that many young men view basic training as a rite of passage into full manhood. They believe the army when it promises to remake them into superb physical specimens, and are disappointed when this is not the result.

Bourne (1967, p. 195) has summarized this type of socialization well.

The process of basic training is unique in American society, as it represents the only instance when individuals can be forcibly confined against their will, and compelled to perform certain tasks, for other than medical or punitive reasons. It also represents the most radical attempt to change identity and behavior that the average person will encounter.

This account of basic training roughly corresponds to Stages 1 and 2 of the model developed here, with the beginning of events located in Stage 3 (such as (a) and (b)). Clearly, however, the recruits will need to be in the army much longer to encounter the remaining two events of Stage 3 and those associated with Stage 4.

SOCIALIZATION AND SELECTION

One way organizations can match newcomers with the work environment is through socialization, i.e., changing the person's role expectations, skills, or motivation. Besides this, two other matching processes were discussed earlier in the book: (1) self-selection through realistic recruitment and (2) selection by the organization.

The relationship between selection and socialization really depends on a third factor—the *type of an organization* that newcomers enter. In some organizations control of the new human inputs is achieved via careful selection, whereas in others much more effort must be directed toward socializing them. Amitai Etzioni (1964), a sociologist, has distinguished among three types of organizations that differ in the "mix" of selection and socialization used to integrate newcomers into the organization. The basis for the three categories is how *control* in the organization is achieved. Control mechanisms are imperative for social organizations because they cannot rely on the inherent cooperation of members.

Etzioni outlines three control mechanisms: physical, material, and symbolic. Physical means, or the threat of their use, are called *coercive* control, e.g., prisons. Organizations using material control are called *utilitarian* organizations, e.g., business is the best example of a utilitarian organization in that it uses financial incentives. Symbolic means do not involve any physical threat nor the use of material incentives. Some symbols, such as prestige and esteem, are normative, while others, such as love and acceptance, are social.

With these three types of control mechanism as the basis, it is possible to see the complex connections between selection and socialization. One major difference among the three organization types is how much each can control its own boundary through being highly selective in the entry of newcomers. At one extreme are the coercive organizations that have virtually no control. Prisons simply accept those sent to them. This means that other control mechanisms are employed on a postentry basis. At the other extreme are utilitarian organizations that often go to great lengths to be highly selective. Within the normative category, there is much more variability; i.e., there is no typical example. There can be as much selectivity of newcomers as in utilitarian organizations, e.g., private schools and Ivy League universities. There can also be as little control over the influx of new members as the two major political parties exert. Figure 6.1 graphically summarizes these relationships.

Etzioni's viewpoint can be summarized as follows: organizational control mechanisms (selection or socialization) are necessary to achieve specific objectives, and selection or socialization can be used as substitutes for each other. Despite the logical appeal of this view, there has been relatively little research designed to test it. One exception to this is a study of civil defense organizations in Minnesota, Georgia, and Massachusetts (Mulford, Klonglan, Beal, and Bohlen 1968).

Civil defense is a normative type of organization, and one that is primarily *moderate* in terms of its control over the entry of newcomers. Despite its generally moderate position with respect to control of newcomer entry, there were differences among the various ($N = 240$) local organizations. The degree of selectivity was measured using the *selection ratio* for each local organization, and they were divided into

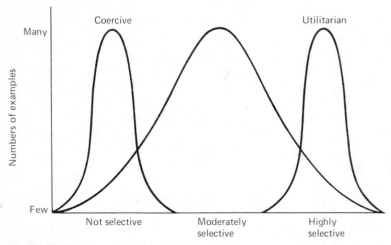

Fig. 6.1 *Degree of "selectivity" for different types of organizations.*

three groups (high–medium–low selectivity) for further analysis. The authors found that

- In general, both selectivity and socialization efforts increase performance.

- However, the effects of socialization on performance is zero for those organizations that were highly selective in the entry of newcomers.

- Socialization efforts increased performance for both the medium and low selective organizations.

A classic approach of what can happen in a utilitarian organization has been documented by Argyris (1954), who studied a medium-size bank in New England. There was relatively little need for extensive indoctrination efforts since the bank selected only those that closely matched a particular profile. Newcomers were uniformly meek, quiet, obedient, tactful, cautious, careful, nonaggressive, submissive, complacent, and security conscious. They all had low self-confidence and were followers rather than leaders. From an organizational perspective this degree of homogeneity made it possible for the bank to continue its implicit "caste system." The officer group was assured of relatively little challenge from within. The other major effect of this hiring policy was on how loan prospects were evaluated— they were judged according to the same criteria as were new employees.

In a follow-up to the original Argyris study, Alderfer (1971) found that many changes in the *selection* function resulted in the institution of a management training program for newcomers (an example of socialization). Several mergers had occurred, new services were added, and the sources for newcomers were expanded to include industries outside banking, e.g., finance companies, sales and advertising agencies, and data processing companies. Thus the organization became much more active in its attempts to socialize newcomers because its highly selective control over the entry of newcomers was curtailed. The program lasted 33 weeks during which each newcomer spent some time in each of the bank's major departments. During this time each trainee was assigned a "big brother," who was a former graduate of this program.

The final way in which selectivity and socialization interact is through the newcomer's preentry experiences. One example of this is the way some newcomers are socialized by the type of professional training received in school, and another is the way newcomers self-select themselves into particular occupations.

Much has been written about the entry of professionally trained newcomers into organizations and the issue of where the loyalties of these newcomers ultimately lie. The issue is whether a professional will be able to closely identify with the employing organization (and be a "local"), or whether a professional will remain identified with the larger group of similar professionals (and be a "cosmopolitan"), as originally discussed by Gouldner (1957, 1958) For many years the need to socialize professionals has been considered important. Socialization of professionals is sometimes seen as the "antidote" to extensive preentry, *professional* socialization. More recently, however, others have taken a different view. This view is that socialization in one's profession is primarily reflected in one's *self-selection* into an organization. A study of 390 aerospace engineers found that those with Ph.D.'s gravitated toward basic research while those with master's degrees went into applied research units (Miller and Wager 1971). These authors argue that the basic "cosmopolitan versus local" orientation is set *prior* to entry during professional training. Then when newcomers self-select into particular jobs, they choose matching parts of the organization. The net effects of this self-selection process are to reduce the potential for individual versus organization conflict and to reduce the need for extensive socialization attempts by the organization.

MATCHING INDIVIDUAL AND ORGANIZATION

One consistent theme running throughout this book has concerned the matching of individual and organization. The Matching Model used here clearly shows the two basic ways in which this can be done. The specific methods to effect better matches have been discussed under the topics of realistic recruitment, organizational choice, organizational selection, and socialization of newcomers.

The idea of matching the individual's abilities to job requirements has been endorsed by most people. The concept of matching human needs to organizational climates has been advocated here, but some have expressed concern that there might be problems with "too much" matching of person to organization. Argyris (1954, 1957) raised this possibility in his study (mentioned earlier) of a New England bank. He found that the bank's selection and socialization procedures ensured that newcomers were very similar to the bank's concept of the "right type." In Argyris's opinion this was simply too much matching, with the consequence of high conformity among newcomers. The personal and organizational risk taking that often leads to creativity was not happening at the bank.

Schein (1968) has also been concerned that too much matching between the individual's needs and the organization's climates will lead to low levels of innovation. Schein has identified two types of organizational norms, pivotal and relevant, to which individuals may (or may not) be matched.

Pivotal norms and values are the most basic ones in an organization, e.g., profit motive in business, service to others in hospitals, knowledge and teaching in schools, and belief in a deity in religious establishments. Other examples from a business organization include belief in the free enterprise system, competition, and a hierarchy of authority as a way to get things done. In contrast, acceptance of *relevant* norms and values are not absolutely necessary as the price of organizational membership. Examples of relevant norms include certain types of dress codes, standards for one's public behavior, expectations about where one ought to live, views about what political beliefs to hold, and finally, what clubs should be joined. The hypothetical relationship between acceptance–rejection of the pivotal and relevant values is shown in Fig. 6.2 in terms of its impact on the amount of innovation likely to result from each of the three matches.

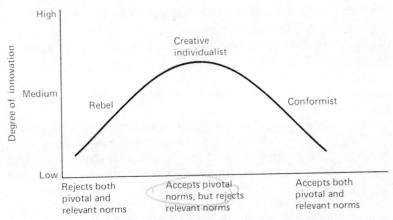

Fig. 6.2 *Possible relationship between different matches and innovation. (Adapted from E. H. Schein, 1968, Organizational socialization and the profession of management,* Industrial Management Review *9: 1–16.)*

The two extreme cases, the Rebel and the Conformist, should be avoided if the organization is to have a vital changing structure and climate, according to Schein. Conformists are typically low in the amount of innovative activity. Rebels may or may not be innovative. When they are, their innovativeness is used *against* pivotal organizational values and norms.

Two notes of caution should probably be made with respect to Schein's appealing idea. First, in any organization there are likely to be all three types, with the conformists being the largest group. Schein does not specify how much conformity is too much, nor how many creative individualists it takes to keep the organization moving. Second, Schein's argument is based mostly on its logical appeal; i.e., he does not offer concrete data from organizations in support of it.

There have, however, been four studies that directly evaluated the results of matching people and organizations. First, a study of 1,852 nursing students in 43 different schools (Katzell 1968) used two questionnaires to measure initial expectations and to measure actual experiences eight months later. The more a nursing student's expectations were confirmed by experience, the less likely was the student to drop out of the program.

A second study involved 90 graduates of the M.I.T. Sloan School of Management (Kotter 1973) also used a questionnaire to assess the degree of matches in expectations. The term "psychological contract" was used in this study as the reference to *mutual* expectations being met: (1) the individual's expectations about what the organization will do, and (2) the organization's expectations about what the individual will do. The major findings of this study are shown in Fig. 6.3. Quite a number of positive outcomes was realized as a result of close matches between the individual and organization.

A third example is an experimental study by Morse (1975) testing the matching idea by comparing the results of placing on jobs one group of newcomers who were well-matched (both in skills and in needs) and placing on jobs another group of newcomers according to the traditional method (concern for skills only). After eight months on the jobs it became clear that the 85 people who were matched by skills *and* needs were more satisfied and felt more competent than did the 50 persons who were matched by skills only. Because of its experimental nature, this study is probably the best example of the results likely to occur from matching newcomers in *both* ways specified by the Matching Model.

The only study that did not find strong results in support of the Matching Model was conducted in the life insurance industry (Schneider 1975). This study found mixed results. Through previous research, four different types of agencies were identified. The matching of individual needs to the climates of the agency was *un*related to job performance (sales) and to turnover for all agencies, except the *worst* one. In this case the worse the individual was matched, the better the performance and the lower the turnover. The moral to this study seems to be "If you have a 'sick' organization, do *not* recruit newcomers similar to those already in your organization. To do so would seem only to perpetuate ineffectiveness."

The results of Schneider's study fit nicely with the cautions about too much matching raised by Argyris and Schein. A more precise way to state the reservation about the matching process is to consider the past and current performance of an organization. Ineffective organizations do not need "more of the same" if they are to improve. So, matching newcomers to the organization may have to be closely scrutinized to see if conformity is a factor in low performance. Should this turn out to be the case, new criteria for matching newcomers must be developed. On the other hand, effective organizations are likely to continue the matching process, and they are justified in doing so.

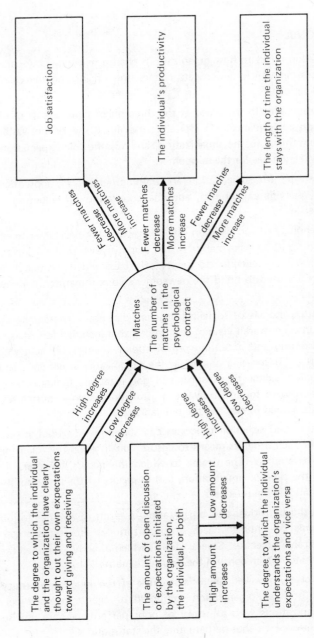

Fig. 6.3 *Impact of matching expectations. (From J. Kotter, 1975,* The Psychological Contract, *p. 95. Copyright © 1975 by the Regents of the University of California. Reprinted from California Management Review 15 (3): 95, by permission of the Regents.)*

CONCLUSIONS

1. Socialization refers to how organizations change newcomers. A parallel process in which newcomers change the organization is called personalization.

2. Socialization efforts are aimed at the three major components of effective job performance: (1) job-relevant skills, (2) work motivation and commitment to the organization, and (3) the role expectations the organization has for the newcomer.

3. Five strategies for socialization are training, education, apprenticeship, debasement experiences, and the cooptation or seduction of newcomers.

4. The psychology of socialization involves getting the newcomer to expend effort and to make many "small" commitments to the organization. The human tendency to justify effort expended and decisions made is then used to build the newcomer's commitment to the new organization.

5. Several stage models of socialization were discussed. These were integrated into an overall view of this process that included four stages: (1) confronting and accepting organizational reality, (2) achieving role clarity, (3) locating oneself in the organizational context, and (4) detecting signposts of successful socialization. Similarities in socialization were found in diverse organizations such as businesses, schools, the armed forces, and the police force.

6. Socialization and selection processes can sometimes be used as substitutes for each other as means to ensure "quality control" over the input of newcomers. The degree to which this occurs, however, depends on the *type* of organization, and in particular the permeability of organizational boundaries.

7. Matching the individual and organization in terms of abilities to job requirements, and human needs to organizational climates is a generally desirable objective. Several studies which directly examined the needs–climates match confirm the positive benefits to be gained.

8. In some cases, however, there is the risk of too much conformity stemming from an organization composed of overly matched persons. Organizations with a history of poor performance are unwise to match newcomers thus perpetuating the status quo.

Bibliography

Adams, J. S., 1963. Toward an understanding of inequity. *Journal of Abnormal and Social Psychology* **67**: 422–436.

Adams, S., 1974. How to charm the campus recruiter. *MBA Magazine,* November.

Anastasi, A., 1968. *Psychological Testing* (3rd ed.), New York: Macmillan.

Alderfer, C. P., 1971. Effect of individual, group, and intergroup relations on attitudes toward a management development program. *Journal of Applied Psychology* **55**: 302–311.

_____, 1972. *Existence, Relatedness and Growth: Human Needs in Organizational Settings.* New York: Free Press.

_____, and C. G. McCord, 1972. Personal and situational factors in the recruitment interview. *Journal of Applied Psychology* **54**: 377–385.

Argyris, C., 1954. *Organization of a Bank.* New Haven: Yale Labor and Management Center.

_____, 1957. *Personality and Organization.* New York: Harper.

_____, 1964. *Integrating the Individual and the Organization.* New York: Wiley.

Aronson, E., 1972. *The Social Animal.* San Francisco: Freeman.

Arvey, R. D., 1979. *Fairness in Employee Selection.* Reading, Mass.: Addison-Wesley.

Ash, P., and L. P. Kroeker, 1975. Personnel selection, classification, and placement. *Annual Review of Psychology* **26**: 481–508.

Asher, J. J., and J. A. Sciarrino, 1974. Realistic work sample tests: A review. *Personnel Psychology* **27**: 519–533.

Bakke, E. W., 1953. *The Fusion Process.* New Haven: Yale University, Labor and Management Center.

Bem, D. J., 1970. *Beliefs, Attitudes, and Human Affairs.* Belmont, Calif.: Brooks/Cole.

Berlew, D. E., and D. T. Hall, 1966. The socialization of managers: effects of expectations on performance. *Administrative Science Quarterly* **11**: 207–223.

Blau, P. M., J. W. Gustad, R. Jesson, H. S. Parnes, and R. C. Wilcox, 1956. Occupational choices: a conceptual framework. *Industrial and Labor Relations Review* **9**: 531, 536–537, 543.

Blum, M. L., and J. C. Naylor, 1968. *Industrial Psychology: Its Theoretical and Social Foundations* (rev. ed.). New York: Harper & Row.

Bourne, P. G., 1967. Some observations on the psychosocial phenomena seen in basic training. *Psychiatry* **30**: 187–197.

Bray, D. W., 1978. The AT&T assessment center program. Talk given at the annual meeting of the Academy of Management Association, San Francisco.

———, R. J. Campbell, and D. L. Grant, 1974. *Formative Years in Business.* New York: Wiley.

Brayfield, A. H., and W. H. Crockett, 1955. Employee attitudes and performance, *Psychological Bulletin* **52**: 396–428.

Brim, O. G., Jr., and S. Wheeler, 1966. *Socialization after Childhood: Two Essays.* New York: Wiley.

Buchanan, B., 1974. Building organizational commitment: the socialization of managers in work organizations. *Administrative Science Quarterly* **19**: 533–546.

Caplow, T., 1964. *Principles of Organization.* New York: Harcourt, Brace and World.

Cherrington, D. J., H. J. Reitz, and W. E. Scott, 1971. Effects of contingent and noncontingent reward on the relationship between satisfaction and task performance. *Journal of Applied Psychology* **55**: 331–336.

Cohen, P., 1973. *The Gospel According to the Harvard Business School.* Garden City, N.Y.: Doubleday and Company.

Connolly, T., and C. V. Vines, 1977. Some instrumentality–valence models of undergraduate college choice. *Decision Sciences* 8: 311–317.

Crites, J. O., 1969. *Vocational Psychology.* New York: McGraw-Hill.

Crooks, L. A., 1977. The selection and development of assessment center techniques. In J. L. Moses and W. C. Byham (eds.), *Applying the Assessment Center Method.* Elmsford, N.Y.: Pergamon Press.

Decker, P. J., and E. T. Cornelius III, 1979. A note on recruiting sources and job survival rates. *Journal of Applied Psychology* 69: 463–464.

Downs, S., R. M. Farr, and L. Colbeck, 1978. Self-appraisal: a convergence of selection and guidance. *Journal of Occupational Psychology* 51: 271–278.

Dunnette, M. D., 1966. *Personnel Selection and Placement.* Belmont, Calif.: Wadsworth.

_____, (ed.), 1976. *Handbook of Industrial and Organizational Psychology.* Chicago: Rand McNally.

_____, R. D. Arvey, and P. A. Banas, 1973. Why do they leave? *Personnel* 50 (3): 25–39.

Egbert, L., G Battit, C. Welch, and M. Bartlett, 1964. Reduction of post-operative pain by encouragement and instruction of patients. *New England Journal of Medicine* 270: 825–827.

Etzioni, A., 1964. *Modern Organizations.* Englewood Cliffs, N.J.: Prentice-Hall.

Farr, J. L., B. S. O'Leary, and C. J. Bartlett, 1973. Effect of a work sample test upon self-selection and turnover of job applicants. *Journal of Applied Psychology* 58: 283–285.

Feldman, D. C., 1976a. A contingency theory of socialization. *Administrative Science Quarterly* 21: 433–452.

_____, 1976b. A practical program for employee socialization. *Organizational Dynamics* (Autumn): 64–80.

Feron, J., 1977. West Point will revise its policies on finding and training women. *New York Times,* April 17.

Festinger, L., 1954. A theory of social comparison processes. *Human Relations* 7: 117-140.

_____, 1957. A theory of cognitive dissonance. Evanston, Ill.: Row, Peterson.

Flamholtz, E. G., 1972. Toward a theory of human resource value in formal organizations. *The Accounting Review* 47: 666-678.

Flanagan, J. C., 1954. The critical incident technique. *Psychological Bulletin* 51: 327-358.

Foltman, F., 1968. *White and Blue Collars in a Mill Shutdown.* Ithaca, N.Y.: New York State School of Industrial and Labor Relations.

Forrest, C. R., L. L. Cummings, and A. C. Johnson, 1977. Organizational participation: a critique and model. *Academy of Management Review* 2: 586-601.

Frederickson, N., D. R. Saunders, and B. Wand, 1957. The in-basket test. *Psychological Monographs* 71(9, Whole No. 438).

Gannon, M. J., 1971. Sources of referral and employee turnover. *Journal of Applied Psychology* 55: 226-228.

Ghiselli, E. E., 1966. *The Validity of Occupational Aptitude Tests.* New York: Wiley.

_____, 1973. The validity of aptitude tests in personnel selection. *Personnel Psychology* 26: 461-478.

Glueck, W. F., 1974. Decision making: organizational choice. *Personnel Psychology* 27: 77-93.

Goldstein, I. I., 1974. *Training: Program Development and Evaluation.* Belmont, Calif.: Wadsworth.

Gomersall, E. R., and M. S. Myers, 1966. Breakthrough in on-the-job training. *Harvard Business Review,* July-August, pp. 62-72.

Gouldner, A. W., 1957. Cosmopolitans and locals: toward an analysis of latent social roles—I. *Administrative Science Quarterly* 2: 281-306.

_____, 1958. Cosmopolitans and locals: toward an analysis of latent social roles—II. *Administrative Science Quarterly* 2: 444-480.

Guion, R. M., 1965. *Personnel Testing.* New York: McGraw-Hill.

Haccoun, R. R., 1978. The effects of realistic job previews and their position within the selection sequence on telephone operator behavior and attitudes. Unpublished manuscript, University of Montreal.

Hackman, J. R., 1977. Work design. In J. R. Hackman and J. L. Suttle (eds.) *Improving Life at Work.* Santa Monica Calif.: Goodyear.

_____, and C. G. Morris, 1975. Group tasks, group interaction process, and group performance effectiveness: a review and proposed integration. In L. Berkowitz (ed.), *Advances in Experimental Social Psychology* (Vol. 8), pp. 45–99. New York: Academic Press.

Hackman, J. R., and G. R. Oldham, 1974a. *The Job Diagnostic Survey: An Instrument for the Diagnosis of Jobs and the Evaluation of Job Redesign Projects.* New Haven: Yale University, School of Organization and Management, Technical Report 4, May.

_____, 1974b. *Motivation through the Design of Work: Test of a Theory.* New Haven: Yale University, Department of Administrative Sciences, Technical Report 6, December.

_____, 1975. Development of the job diagnostic survey. *Journal of Applied Psychology* **60**: 159–170.

_____, 1980. *Work Redesign.* Reading, Mass.: Addison-Wesley.

Hall, D. T., 1976. *Careers in Organizations.* Pacific Palisades, Calif.: Goodyear.

_____, and S. Rabinowitz, 1977. Organizational research on job involvement. *Psychological Bulletin* **84**: 265–288.

Heneman, H. G., Jr., H. Fox, and D. Yoder, 1948. Patterns of manpower mobility: Minneapolis, 1948. In D. Yoder and D. G. Paterson (eds.), *Local Labor Market Research.* Minneapolis: Univeristy of Minnesota Press.

Herzberg, F. H., 1968. One more time: how do you motivate employees? *Harvard Business Review* **46**: 53–62.

_____, B. Mausner, R. O. Peterson, and D. F. Capwell, 1957. *Job Attitudes: A Review of Research and Opinion.* Pittsburgh: Psychological Service of Pittsburgh.

Hinrichs, J. R., 1978. An eight-year follow-up of a management assessment center. *Journal of Applied Psychology* **63**: 596–601.

Hoffman, L. R., 1965. Group problem solving. In L. Berkowitz (ed.), *Advances in Experimental Social Psychology* (Vol. II), pp. 99–132. New York: Academic Press.

Hoiberg, A., and N. H. Berry 1978. Expectations and perceptions of Navy life. *Organizational Behavior and Human Performance* **21**: 130–145.

Holmes, D. S., 1977. How and why assessment works. In J. L. Moses and W. C. Byham (eds.), *Applying the Assessment Center Model*. Elmsford, N.Y.: Pergamon.

Horner, S. O., 1979. *The Effects of Expectations through Realistic Job Previews (RJPs) on Marine Corps Attrition.* Paper presented at the annual meeting of the American Psychological Association, September.

Howard, A., 1974. An assessment of assessment centers. *Academy of Management Journal* **17**: 115–134.

Ilgen, D. R., and B. L. Dugoni, 1977. *Initial Orientation to the Organization.* Paper presented at the annual meeting of the Academy of Management Association, August.

Ilgen, D. R., and W. Seely, 1974. Realistic expectations as an aid in reducing voluntary resignations. *Journal of Applied Psychology* **59**: 452–455.

Ivancevich, J. M., and J. M. Donnelly, 1971. Job offer acceptance behavior and reinforcement. *Journal of Applied Psychology* **55**: 119–122.

Janis, I. L., and L. Mann, 1977. *Decision Making: A Psychological Analysis of Conflict, Choice, and Commitment.* New York: Free Press.

———, and D. Wheeler, 1978. Thinking clearly about career choices. *Psychology Today* May: 67 ff.

Janz, J. T., and M. D. Dunnette, 1977. An approach to selection decisions: dollars and sense. In J. R. Hackman, E. E. Lawler, III, and L. W. Porter (eds.), *Perspectives on Behavior in Organizations.* New York: McGraw-Hill, pp. 119–126.

Jeswald, Thomas A., 1977. Issues in establishing an assessment center. In J. L. Moses and W. C. Byham (eds.), *Applying the Assessment Center Method.* Elmsford, N. Y.: Pergamon, pp. 45–66.

Johnson, J. E., 1966. The influence of purposeful nurse–patient interaction on the patient's postoperative course. *A.N.A. Monograph Series*

2. *Exploring Medical-Surgical Nursing Practice.* New York: American Nurses Association.

_____, and H. Leventhal, 1974. Effects of accurate expectations and behavioral instructions on reactions during a noxious medical examination. *Journal of Personality and Social Psychology* **29**: 710–718.

Katz, D., and R. L. Kahn, 1966. *The Social Psychology of Organizations.* New York: Wiley.

Katzell, M. E., 1968. Expectations and dropouts in schools of nursing. *Journal of Applied Psychology* **52**: 154–157.

Kerr, C., 1942. Migration to the Seattle labor market area, 1940–1942. *University of Washington Publications in the Social Sciences* **11**: 151, note 1 August 1942.

Klimoski, R. J., and W. J. Strickland, 1977. Assessment centers—valid or merely prescient. *Personnel Psychology* **30**: 353–361.

Korman, A. K., 1977. *Organizational Behavior.* Englewood Cliffs, N.J.: Prentice-Hall.

Kotter, J., 1973. The psychological contract. *California Management Review* **15** (3): 91–99.

Krausz, M., and S. Fox 1979. The impact of different types of realistic previews upon initial expectations, expectation fulfillment, satisfaction, and withdrawal rates. Unpublished manuscript, Department of Labour Studies, Tel Aviv University.

Latham, G. P., and K. N. Wexley, 1977. Behavioral observation scales for performance appraisal purposes. *Personnel Psychology* **30**: 255–268.

Lawler, E. E., III, 1971. *Pay and Organizational Effectiveness: A Psychological View.* New York: McGraw-Hill.

_____, 1973. *Motivation in Work Organizations.* Monterey, Calif.: Brooks/Cole.

_____, W. J. Kuleck, J. G. Rhode, and J. E. Sorenson, 1975. Job choice and post decision dissonance. *Organizational Behavior and Human Performance* **13**: 133–145.

Levy, J. M., and R. K. McGee, 1975. Childbirth as crisis: a test of Janis's theory of communication and stress resolution. *Journal of Personality and Social Psychology* **31**: 171–179.

Lewicki, R. J., 1978. A theory of organizational seduction. Unpublished manuscript, Durham, N. C.: Duke University, Graduate School of Business Administration.

Lewin, A. Y., and A. Zwany, 1976. Peer nominations: a model, literature critique and a paradigm for research. *Personnel Psychology* **29**: 423–447.

Lewis, M., 1965. Psychological effect of effort. *Psychological Bulletin* **64**: 183–190.

LIMRA, Research Report, 1962–1966. *Source Mix and Source Performance.* Hartford, Conn.: Life Insurance Marketing and Research Association.

Locke, E. A., 1968. Toward a theory of task motivation and incentives. *Organizational Behavior and Human Performance* **3**: 157–189.

Lofquist, L. H., and R. V. Dawis, 1969. *Adjustment to Work.* New York: Appleton-Century-Crofts.

McClelland, D. C., J. W. Atkinson, R. A. Clark, and E. L. Lowell, 1953. *The Achievement Motive.* New York: Appleton-Century-Crofts.

McCormick, E. J., and J. Tiffin, 1974. *Industrial Psychology* (6th ed.). Englewood Cliffs, N. J.: Prentice-Hall.

Macedonia, R. M., 1969. *Expectations—Press and Survival.* Unpublished doctoral dissertation, New York: New York University.

McGuire, W. J., 1964. Inducing resistance to persuasion. In L. Berkowitz (ed.), *Advances in Experimental Social Psychology* (Vol. III). New York: Academic Press.

Malm, F. T., 1954. Recruiting patterns and the functioning of labor markets. *Industrial and Labor Relations Review* **7**: 507–525.

March, J. G., and H. A. Simon, 1958. *Organizations.* New York: Wiley.

Marchese, T. J. 1976. *Barat—A Prospectus, 1976-1977.* Lake Forest, Ill.: Barat College.

Marrow, A. J., D. G. Bowers, and S. E. Seashore, 1967. *Management by Participation.* New York: Harper & Row.

Maslow, A. H. 1943. A theory of human motivation. *Psychological Review* **50**: 370–396.

Mayfield, E. C., 1964. The selection interview: A re-evaluation of published research. *Personnel Psychology* **17**: 239-260.

Miller, G. A., and L. W. Wager, 1971. Adult socialization, organizational structure, and role orientations. *Administrative Science Quarterly* **16**: 151-163.

Miller, J. C., and N. Treiger, 1977. Personal and situational determinants of presurgical stress. Unpublished manuscript cited by I. L. Janis and L. Mann in *Decision Making*. New York: Free Press.

Mintzberg, H., 1973. *The Nature of Managerial Work.* New York: Harper & Row.

Mirvis, P. H., and E. E. Lawler, III, 1977. Measuring the financial impact of employee attitudes. *Journal of Applied Psychology* **62**: 1-8.

Mobley, W. H., R. W. Griffeth, H. H. Hand, and B. M. Meglino, 1979. Review and conceptual analysis of the employee turnover process. *Psychological Bulletin* **86**: 493-522.

Moore, M. L., 1974. Superior, self, and subordinate differences in perceptions of managerial learning times. *Personnel Psychology* **27**: 297-305.

Moran, P. A., 1963. *An Experimental Study of Pediatric Admission.* New Haven: Yale University School of Nursing.

Morse, J. J., 1975. Person-job congruence and individual adjustment. *Human Relations* **28**: 841-861.

Moses, J. L., and W. C. Byham, (eds.), 1977. *Applying the Assessment center method.* Elmsford, N. Y.: Pergamon.

Mulford, C. L., G. E. Klonglan, G. N. Beal, and J. M. Bohlen, 1968. Selectivity, socialization, and role performance. *Sociology and Social Research* **53** (1): 68-77.

Myers, C. A., and W. R. MacLaurin, 1943. *The Movement of Factory Workers: A Study of a New England Industrial Community.* New York: Wiley.

Myers, C. A., and G. P. Shultz, 1951. *The Dynamics of a Labor Market.* Englewood Cliffs, N.J.: Prentice-Hall.

Nadler, D. A., and E. E. Lawler, III, 1977. Motivation: a diagnostic approach. In J. R. Hackman, E. E. Lawler, III, and L. W. Porter (eds.), *Perspectives on Behavior in Organizations.* New York: McGraw-Hill.

Nicholson, H., C. A. Brown, and J. K. Chadwick-Jones, 1976. Absence from work and job satisfaction. *Journal of Applied Psychology* **61**: 728–737.

Nissen, B., 1978. At Texas Instruments, if you're pro-union, firm may be anti-you. *Wall Street Journal,* July 28, p. 1.

The Office of Strategic Services Assessment Staff, 1948. *Assessment of Men.* New York: Rinehart.

Oldham, G. R., 1976. Organizational choice, and some correlates of individuals' expectancies. *Decision Sciences* **7**: 873–884.

Osburn, H. C., and S. W. Constantin, 1977. The selection interview: some issues raised by research on decision making. Unpublished manuscript.

Parker, D. F., and L. Dyer, 1976. Expectancy theory as a within-person behavioral choice model: an empirical test of some conceptual and methodological refinements. *Organizational Behavior and Human Performance* **17**: 97–117.

Parkington, J. J., and B. Schneider, 1978. A laboratory study of some effects of a realistic task preview. Research Report 17, May. Department of Psychology, University of Maryland.

Parnes, H. S., 1954. *Research on Labor Mobility: An Appraisal of Research Findings in the United States.* New York: Social Science Research Council.

———, 1970. Labor force and labor markets. In *A Review of Industrial Relations Research* (Vol. I). Madison, Wisc.: University of Wisconsin, Industrial Relations Research Association.

Pieters, G. R., A. T. Hundert, and M. Beer, 1968. Predicting organizational choice: a post hoc analysis. *Proceedings of the 76th Annual Convention of the American Psychological Association* **3**: 573–574.

Porter, L. W., W. J. Crampon, and F. J. Smith, 1976. Organizational commitment and managerial turnover: a longitudinal study. *Organizational Behavior and Human Performance* **15**: 87–98.

Porter, L. W., E. E. Lawler, III, and J. R. Hackman, 1975. *Behavior in Organizations.* New York: McGraw-Hill.

Porter, L. W., and R. M. Steers, 1973. Organizational, work, and personal factors in employee turnover and absenteeism. *Psychological Bulletin* **80**: 151–176.

Price, J. L., 1977. *The Study of Turnover.* Ames, Iowa: Iowa State University Press.

Rees, A., 1966. Information networks in labor markets. *American Economic Review,* Papers and Proceedings, May: 559, 562.

Reid, G. L., 1972. Job search and the effectiveness of job-finding methods. *Industrial and Labor Relations Review* **25**: 479–495.

Reilly, R. R., M. L. Tenopyr, and S. M. Sperling, 1979. Effects of job previews on job acceptance and survival of telephone operator candidates. *Journal of Applied Psychology* **64**: 218–220.

Reynolds, L. G., 1951. *The Structure of Labor Markets.* New York: Harper Bros.

Rice, B., 1978. Measuring executive muscle. *Psychology Today* **12** (December): 95–110.

Ryans, D. G., and N. Fredericksen, 1971. Performance tests of educational achievement. In W. W. Ronan and E. P. Prien (eds.) *Perspectives on the Measurement of Human Performance.* New York: Appleton-Century-Crofts.

Salipante, P., and P. S. Goodman, 1976. Training, counseling, and retention of the hard-core unemployed. *Journal of Applied Psychology* **61**: 1–11.

Schein, E. H., 1964. How to break in the college graduate. *Harvard Business Review* **42**: 68–76.

———, 1967. Attitude change during management education: a study of organizational influences on student attitudes. *Administrative Science Quarterly* **11**: 601–628.

———, 1968. Organizational socialization and the profession of management. *Industrial Management Review* **9**: 1–16.

———, 1971. The individual, the organization, and the career: a conceptual scheme. *Journal of Applied Behavioral Science* **7**: 401–426.

_____, 1978. *Career Dynamics: Matching Individual and Organizational Needs.* Reading, Mass.: Addison-Wesley.

Schmidt, R. L., 1966. *An Exploratory Study of Nursing and Patient Readiness for Surgery.* Unpublished master's thesis. New Haven: Yale University School of Nursing.

Schmitt, F. E., and P. J. Woolridge, 1973. Psychological preparation for surgical patients. *Nursing Research* 22: 108–116.

Schmitt, N., 1976. Social and situational determinants of interview decisions: implications for the employment interview. *Personnel Psychology* 29: 79–101.

_____, and B. W. Coyle, 1976. Applicant decisions in the employment interview. *Journal of Applied Psychology* 61: 184–192.

Schneider, B., 1975a. Organizational climates: an essay. *Personnel Psychology* 28: 447–481.

_____, 1975b. Organizational climate: individual preferences and organizational realities revisited. *Journal of Applied Psychology* 60: 459–465.

_____, 1976. *Staffing Organizations.* Pacific Palisades, Calif.: Goodyear.

Schuh, A. J., 1967. The predictability of employee tenure: a review of the literature. *Personnel Psychology* 20: 133–152.

Schwab, D. P., and L. L. Cummings, 1970. Theories of performance: a review. *Industrial Relations* 7: 408–430.

de Schweinitz, D., 1932. *How Workers Find Jobs.* Philadelphia: University of Pennsylvania Press.

Sheard, J. L., 1970. Intrasubject prediction of preferences for organization types. *Journal of Applied Psychology* 54: 248–252.

Sheppard, H. L., and A. H. Belitsky, 1966. *The Job Hunt.* Baltimore: Johns Hopkins Press.

Sheridan, J. E., M. D., Richards, and J. W. Slocum, 1975. Comparative analysis of expectancy and heuristic models of decision behavior. *Journal of Applied Psychology* 60: 361–368.

Smith, F., K. H. Roberts, and C. L. Hulin, 1976. Ten-year job satisfaction trends in a stable organization. *Academy of Management Journal* 19: 462–469.

Smith, P. C., L. M. Kendall, and C. L. Hulin, 1969. *The Measurement of Satisfaction in Work and Retirement.* Chicago: Rand McNally, 1969.

Soelberg, P. O., 1967. Unprogrammed decision making. *Industrial Management Review* **8**: 19–29.

Springbett, B. M., 1958. Factors affecting the final decision in the employment interview. *Canadian Journal of Psychology* **12**: 13–22.

Ulrich, L., and D. Trumbo, 1965. The selection interview since 1949. *Psychological Bulletin* **63**: 100–116.

United States Department of Labor, 1972. *Handbook for Analyzing Jobs.* Washington, D. C.: United States Government Printing Office.

Van Maanen, J., 1973. Observations on the making of policemen. *Human Organization* **32**: 407–418.

_____, 1976a. Breaking in: socialization to work. In R. Dubin (ed.), *Handbook of Work, Organization and Society.* Chicago: Rand McNally.

_____, 1976b. Rookie cops and rookie managers. *Wharton Magazine* **1**: 49–55 (b).

Vernon, D. T. A., and D. A. Bigelow, 1974. Effect of information about a potentially stressful situation on responses to stress impact. *Journal of Personality and Social Psychology* **29**: 50–59.

Vroom, V. H., 1964. *Work and Motivation.* New York: Wiley.

_____, 1966. Organizational choice: a study of pre and post decision processes. *Organizational Behavior and Human Performance* **1**: 212–225.

_____, 1970. Industrial social psychology. In G. Lindzey and E. Aronson (eds.), *Handbook of Social Psychology* (Vol. V). Reading, Mass.: Addison-Wesley.

_____, E. L. Deci, 1971. The stability of post decisional dissonance: a follow-up study of the job attitudes of business school graduates. *Organizational Behavior and Human Performance* **6**: 36–49.

Wagner, E. E., 1949. The employment interview: a critical summary. *Personnel Psychology* **2**: 17–46.

Wahba, M., and L. Bridwell, 1976. Maslow reconsidered: a review of research on the need hierarchy theory. *Organizational Behavior and Human Performance* **15**: 212–240.

Wanous, J. P., 1972a. *An Experimental Test of Job Attraction Theory in an Organizational Setting.* Unpublished doctoral dissertation. New Haven: Yale University.

————, 1972b. Occupational preferences: perceptions of valence and instrumentality, and objective data. *Journal of Applied Psychology* **56**: 152–155.

————, 1973. Effects of a realistic job preview on job acceptance, job attitudes, and job survival. *Journal of Applied Psychology* **58**: 327–332.

————, 1974. A causal-correlational analysis of the job satisfaction and performance relationship. *Journal of Applied Psychology* **59**: 139–144.

————, 1975a. A job preview makes recruiting more effective. *Harvard Business Review* **53** (5): 16, 166, 168.

————, 1975b. Tell it like it is at realistic job previews. *Personnel* **52** (4): 50–60.

————, 1975c. *Organizational Entry: The Transition from Outsider to Newcomer to Insider.* (Working Paper 75-14). New York University, Graduate School of Business Administration.

————, 1976. Organizational entry: from naive expectations to realistic beliefs. *Journal of Applied Psychology* **61**: 22–29.

————, 1977. Organizational entry: newcomers moving from outside to inside. *Psychological Bulletin* **84**: 601–618.

————, 1978. Realistic job previews: can a procedure to reduce turnover also influence the relationship between abilities and performance? *Personnel Psychology* **31**: 249–258.

————, T. Keon, and J. C. Latack, 1979. Choosing an organization. Unpublished manuscript, Department of Management, College of Business, Michigan State University.

Wanous, J. P., and E. E. Lawler, III, 1972. Measurement and meaning of job satisfaction. *Journal of Applied Psychology* **56**: 95–105.

Wanous, J. P., S. A. Stumpf, and H. Bedrosian, 1978. *Turnover of New Employees.* Paper presented at the annual meeting of the Academy of Management Association, San Francisco.

————, 1979. Job survival of new employees. *Personnel Psychology* **32**: 651–662.

Wanous, J. P., and A. Zwany, 1977. A cross-sectional test of need hierarchy theory. *Organizational Behavior and Human Performance* **18**: 78–97.

Ward, L. B., and A. G. Athos, 1972. *Student Expectations of Corporate Life: Implications for Management Recruiting.* Boston: Division of Research, Harvard Business School.

Weitz, J. 1956. Job expectancy and survival. *Journal of Applied Psychology* **40**: 245–247.

Wiskoff, M. F., 1977. *Review of Career Expectations Research: Australia, Canada, United Kingdom, and United States.* San Diego: Navy Personnel Research and Development Center, Technical Note 77-9, March.

Wolfer, J. A., and M. A. Visintainer, 1975. Pediatric surgical patients and parents' stress responses and adjustment as a function of psychologic preparation and stress point nursing care. *Nursing Research* **24**: 244–255.

Wollack, S., J. G. Goodale, J. P. Wijting, and P. C. Smith, 1971. Development of the survey of work values. *Journal of Applied Psychology* **55**: 331–338.

Wright, O. R., 1969. Summary of research on the selection interview since 1964. *Personnel Psychology* **22**: 391–413.

Youngberg, C. F., 1963. *An Experimental Study of Job Satisfaction and Turnover in Relation to Job Expectations and Self-expectations.* Unpublished doctoral dissertation. New York: New York University.

Name Index

Subject Index